ROBOTICS

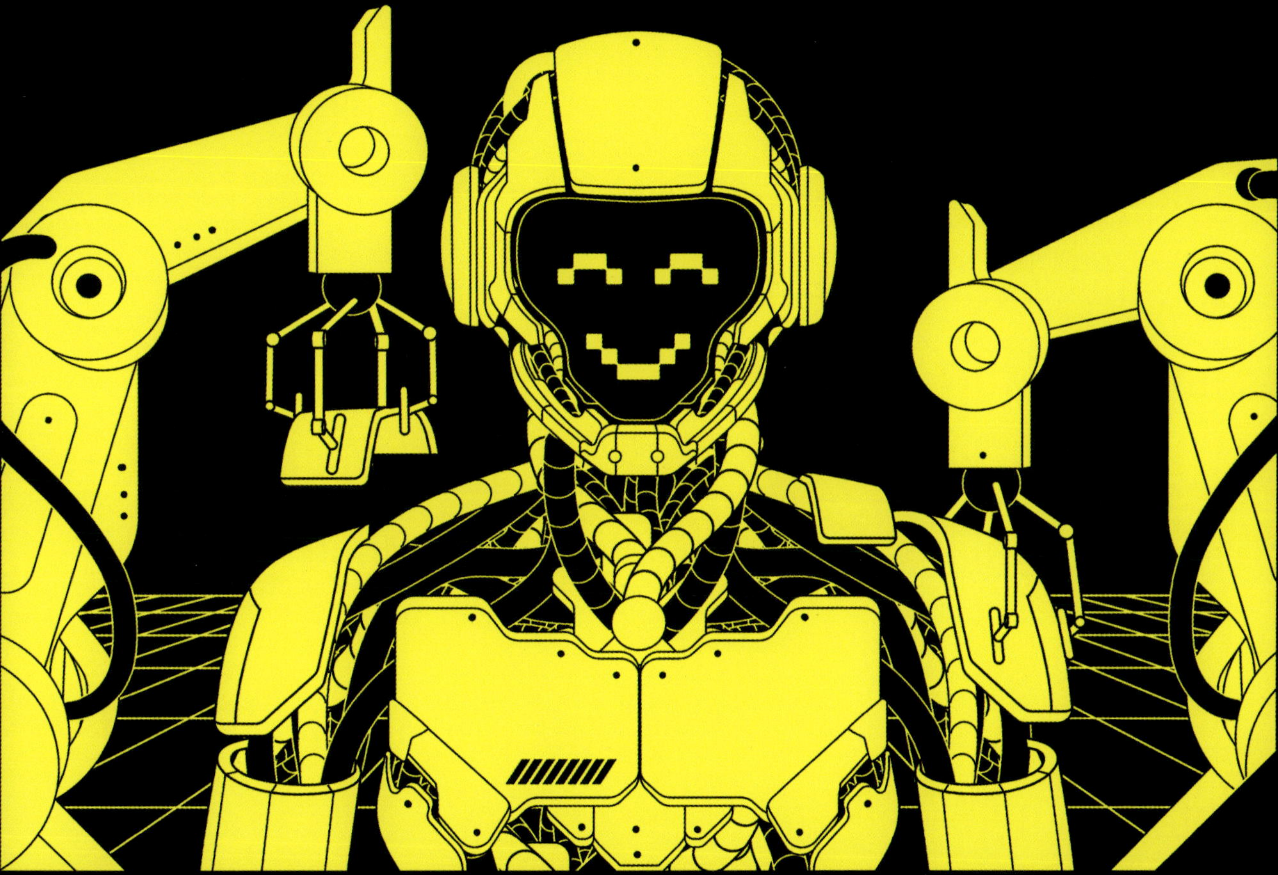

Written by Kate Peridot

Illustrated by Denis Freitas

Contents

The world of robotics.................4
What is a robot?......................6
Autonomous cars....................8
Autonomous trains..................10
Warehouse workers.................12
Shopping with robots...............14
Artificial intelligence................16
Vertical farming.....................18
Large-scale farming................20
Smart farming......................22
Making motor vehicles.............24
Working with people................26
How do robots sense?..............28
Medical robots......................30
Bionic humans......................32
Helpers at home....................34
Clever robots!.......................36
Robotic toys........................38
Ocean conservation................40
Land conservation..................42
Robotic animals....................44
Spider robot........................46
How do robots move?..............48
Military robots......................50
Search and rescue..................52
Robotic mining.....................54
Ocean explorers....................56

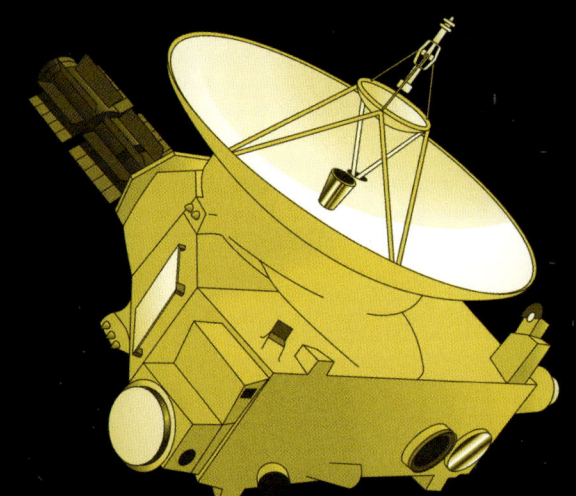

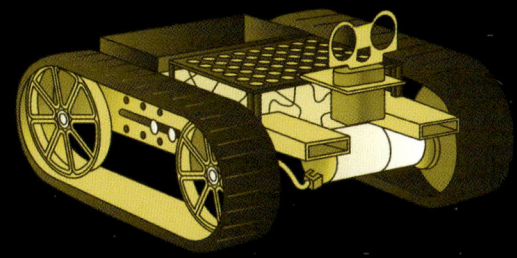

Underwater robots	58
Space robots	60
Talking to astronauts	62
Exploring Mars	64
Space probes	66
The story of robots	68
Step into the future	72
Glossary	74
Index	76
Acknowledgements	80

Project Art Editor Sonny Flynn
Senior Editor Marie Greenwood
Designer Sophie Gordon
Consultant, IPR and Imager Taiyaba Khatoon
Picture Research Administrator Samrajkumar S
Managing Art Editor Diane Peyton Jones
Publisher James Mitchem
Production Editor Becky Fallowfield
Production Controller Joss Moore
Consultants Maurice Fallon, Jared Bellingham

First published in Great Britain in 2025 by
Dorling Kindersley Limited
20 Vauxhall Bridge Road,
London SW1V 2SA

The authorised representative in the EEA is
Dorling Kindersley Verlag GmbH. Arnulfstr. 124,
80636 Munich, Germany

Text copyright © Kate Peridot 2025
Kate Peridot has asserted her right to be identified
as the author of the work
Layout and design copyright © 2025
Dorling Kindersley Limited
A Penguin Random House Company
10 9 8 7 6 5 4 3 2 1
001–351123–Nov/2025

All rights reserved.
No part of this publication may be reproduced, stored in or
introduced into a retrieval system, or transmitted, in any form, or by
any means (electronic, mechanical, photocopying, recording, or
otherwise), without the prior written permission of the copyright
owner. No part of this publication may be used in any manner for
the purpose of training artificial intelligence technologies or systems.
In accordance with Article 4(3) of the DSM Directive
2019/790, DK expressly reserves this work from the text and
data mining exception.
A CIP catalogue record for this book
is available from the British Library.
ISBN: 978-0-2417-5980-6
Printed and bound in China

www.dk.com

This book was made with Forest
Stewardship Council™ certified
paper – one small step in DK's
commitment to a sustainable future.
For more information go to
www.dk.com/uk/information/
sustainability

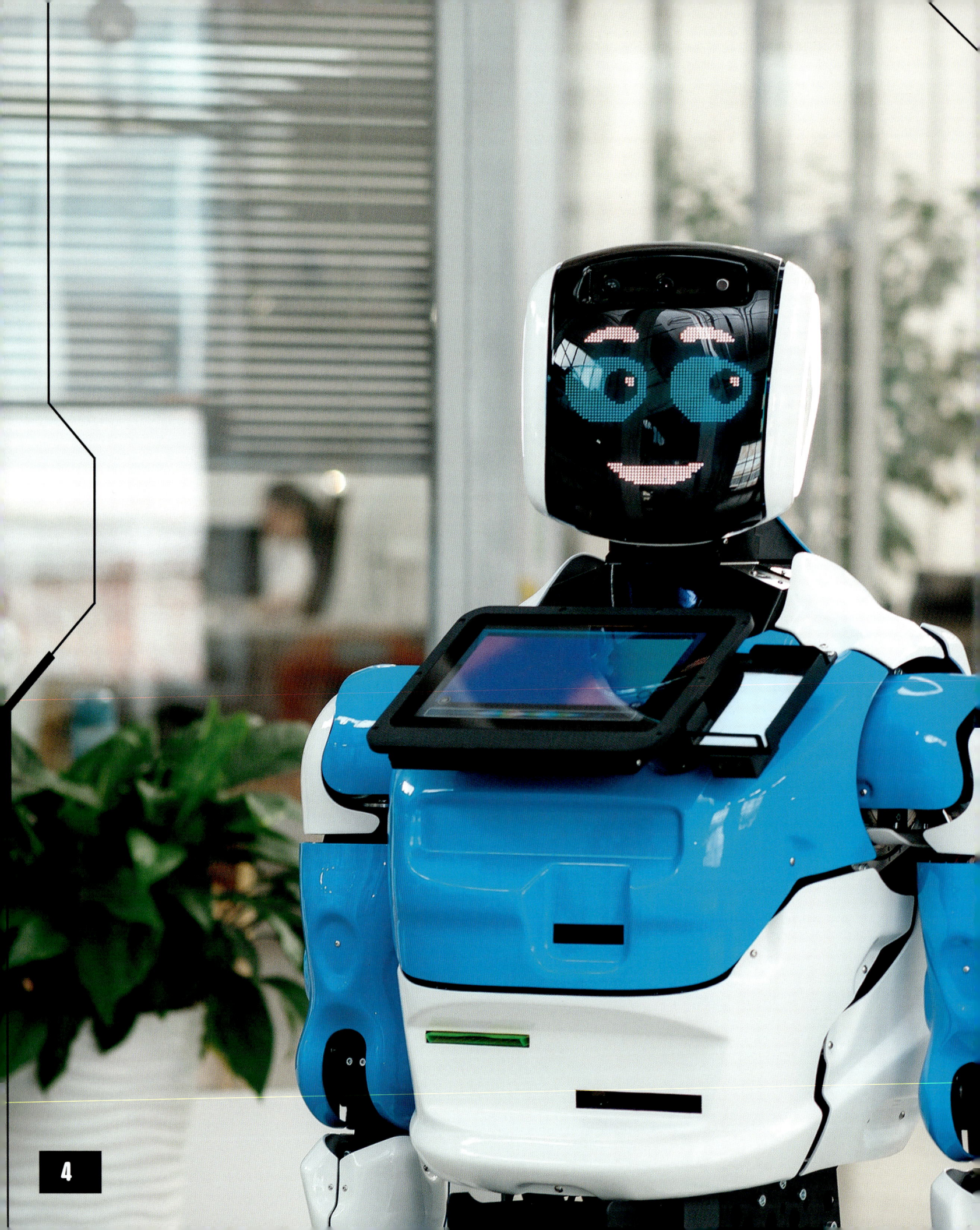

The world of robotics

Robots have long been part of the human imagination. Since ancient times, mechanical beings called automata have appeared in stories and drawings. The word "robot" was first introduced by the Czech playwright, Karel Čapek, in his 1920s play, *R.U.R.: Rossum's Universal Robots*. The Czech word *robota* means "forced labour". Čapek's mechanical workers helped to inspire a new generation of stories and inventions, and "robot" became the word we use today for all robotic machines.

In factories, robots outperform humans by building products with greater speed and precision. On farms, robots plant, water, and harvest crops. In hospitals, they assist doctors during surgeries and provide care for patients. During natural disasters, robots search for survivors and collect information while keeping humans safe. In space, they gather data from distant planets and moons that we can't visit. Robots are also revolutionizing transport, making self-driving cars and trains safer and more reliable. They even teach and play with children and make entertainment more exciting.

Advances in artificial intelligence (AI) are transforming robots into smart teammates capable of working alongside us, communicating, solving problems, and helping us achieve amazing things.

In this book, you'll meet lots of different kinds of robots. Discover how robots understand and perform tasks and the different ways they move. You'll also meet the people who design, engineer, maintain, and use robots in their daily lives.

As technologies continue to advance and become more affordable, robots will soon be a big part of all our lives – at home, in schools, in workplaces, on town and city streets, and even supporting faraway colonies on other planets! As we continue to teach robots to think, learn, and adapt, they become more than just tools; they are helpers and collaborators, shaping a future where humanity and technology move forward together.

The future with robots is full of possibilities!

What is a robot?

Robots are machines that are packed with smart technology. They can sense, compute, and act on their own to complete tasks. Robots come in lots of different shapes and sizes, but most robots have the common parts shown here.

Computer
The robot's computer is its "brain", though the computer's often found in its body, rather than its head! It collects information about the environment from sensors, and stores sets of instructions called programs that tell the robot when and how to move.

Main body
The body of the robot protects the computer, power source, and motor, and houses the sensors and actuators.

Why do we need robots?

- To do tasks we don't want to do, faster and more accurately
- To support and care for us, and to entertain us too
- To go where it's not safe for humans to go
- To think (compute) faster or differently to humans
- To use scientific equipment to explore Earth and the Solar System

Humanoid robot

A humanoid robot looks a bit like you or me! It is especially designed to work alongside humans and is capable of learning and performing a variety of jobs that humans can do – such as lifting and carrying objects, interacting with other humans, and doing repetitive tasks that people might find boring.

Sensors

A robot needs to be able to "sense" the world. A sensor collects information about the environment and sends it to the robot's computer. A robot might have one sensor or many. Electronic sensors collect information in a similar way to human senses. For example, a microphone "hears", a camera "sees", a pressure or tactile sensor "feels", and a smoke detector "smells".

Actuators

A robot's actuators bring it to life. Like muscles in the human body, they convert energy into movement. An actuator might turn a wheel, move a joint on a robotic arm or leg, or activate a tool.

Energy source

Rrobots need an electrical power source to sense, move, and compute. A robot that stays in one place will plug into the main electrical power supply. Robots that move around use rechargeable batteries. Some might have solar panels that convert energy from the Sun to electricity, which charges the batteries.

Main types of robot

Automated robots are simple robots designed and preprogrammed to do one task repetitively. They are often used in factories – for example, to drill or stack products. We humans turn them on and off and adjust their tasks.

Autonomous robots use their sensors to gain knowledge of their environment and use a decision-making process to take the next step without human input. For example, the autonomous robot vacuum cleaner uses sensors to detect dirt, move around objects, and return to its charging station.

Autonomous cars

Autonomous vehicles (AVs) do not have a human driver. The computer drives the vehicle, while passengers sit back and relax. This technology will change the way we travel and could make our busy roads and railways safer, more efficient, and less polluting. AVs look like normal cars, but have added sensors and a computer with AI.

Radar   Cameras   Lidar

Ride-share taxis

The first autonomous ride-sharing vehicles (or robotaxis) are operating in some US cities. Riders use an app on their smartphone to order a taxi. The car arrives, unlocks for the rider to step in and sit down, and drives to the destination. A screen tells passengers what route it will take and when it will arrive. When the power is low, or no one has ordered a ride, the car returns to the depot to park and recharge its batteries.

Lidar (Light Detection and Ranging)

These sensors constantly bounce millions of pulses of light in all directions and measure how long they take to bounce back from objects. This paints a 3D picture of the vehicle's environment, detects road edges and lane markings, and measures distances.

Cameras
Multiple cameras create a 360° view and work in daylight and low light. They are programmed to spot stationary and moving objects 100 m (328 ft) away.

AV tester
To test safety, we place the AV on a track, and put unexpected obstacles in the way. We use driving simulators, which create a virtual training world. Here, we can place a simulated car and test its ability to react properly to a huge variety of challenges and obstacles.

Radar
This bounces radio microwaves towards objects to determine distance and speed. Radar works in rain, fog, and snow.

City transport planner
Imagine everyone owns their own AV or uses an AV ride-share taxi. The AV drops its passenger off at the destination and returns to its own garage. We wouldn't need so many ugly town centre car parks. We could create more green spaces, housing, schools, or shops instead. Operation centres monitor the traffic so AVs could change route to ease road congestion.

Computer
The computer processes information from sensors and identifies different objects. It knows where the car is on a map and plans a safe route towards the destination. AI programming enables the car to know its position, and to make rapid decisions about what it should do next. It also stores information from previous journeys to improve safety and performance.

Autonomous trains

Many cities have at least one autonomous train or tramline. It might link the city to the airport, connect one part of the city to another, or travel to a tourist attraction. Opened in 2002, Copenhagen in Denmark is one of the few cities that has a completely autonomous driverless system of metro trains. Trains run at one-and-a-half-minute intervals during busy times and travel at speeds of up to 80 kph (50 mph).

Driverless trains

Computers can operate driverless trains from a control centre, while still allowing the train some autonomy. Sensors on the trains, track, and signals communicate the location and speed of a train to the control centre. Backup systems step in if anything goes wrong.

London Docklands Light Railway is an elevated railway line that has operated driverless trains since 1987. It connects parts of South and East London.

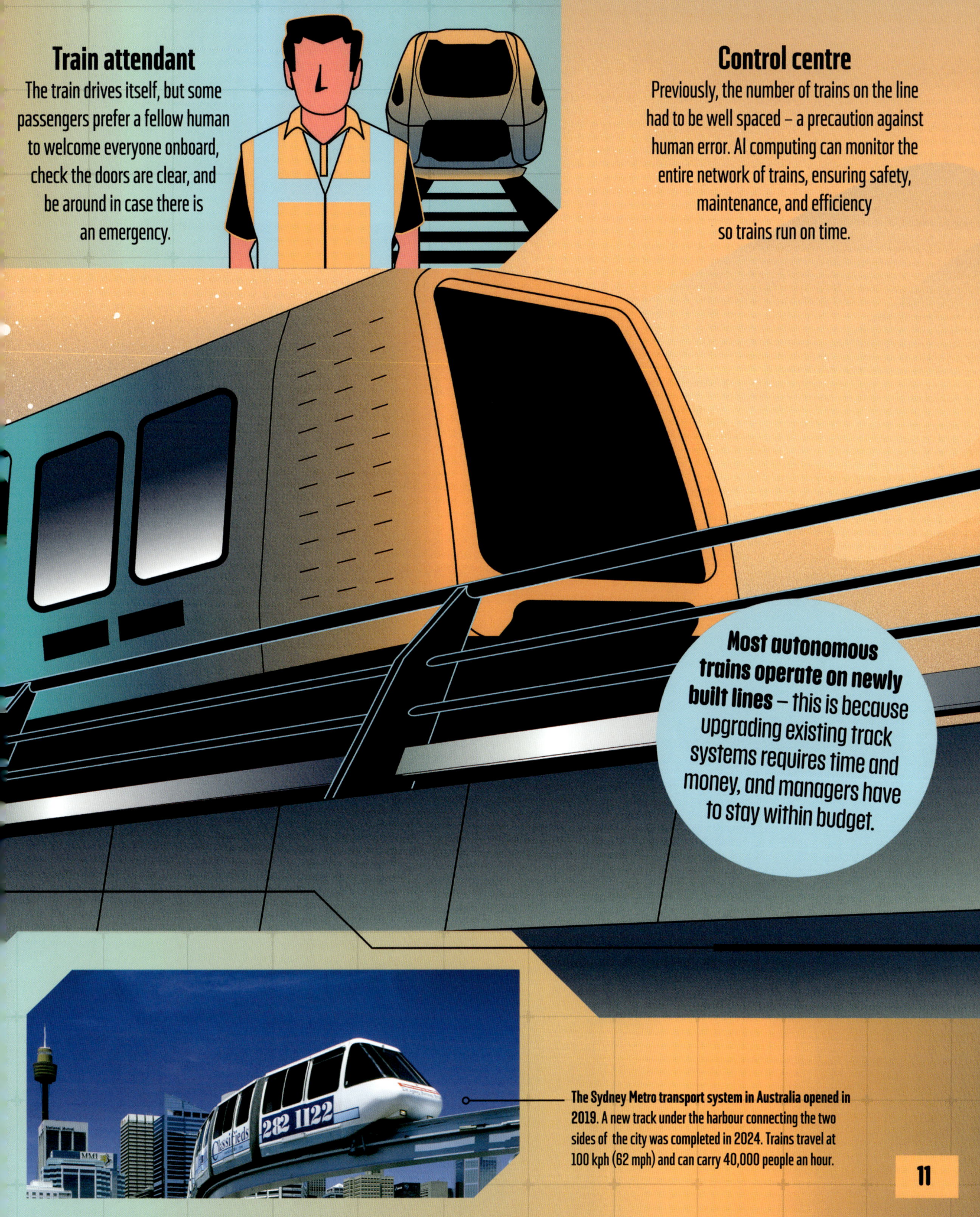

Train attendant
The train drives itself, but some passengers prefer a fellow human to welcome everyone onboard, check the doors are clear, and be around in case there is an emergency.

Control centre
Previously, the number of trains on the line had to be well spaced – a precaution against human error. AI computing can monitor the entire network of trains, ensuring safety, maintenance, and efficiency so trains run on time.

Most autonomous trains operate on newly built lines – this is because upgrading existing track systems requires time and money, and managers have to stay within budget.

The Sydney Metro transport system in Australia opened in 2019. A new track under the harbour connecting the two sides of the city was completed in 2024. Trains travel at 100 kph (62 mph) and can carry 40,000 people an hour.

Warehouse workers

Robots help us shop in lots of different ways. In warehouses, robots count products and restock shelves. They sort, pack, and dispatch goods into trucks for delivery to a store or to a home address.

Stocking and sorting
The online retailer, Amazon, has the largest fleet of industrial robots in the world. Enormous warehouses called fulfilment centres use different types of robots to stock, sort, and dispatch products.

Proteus
The automated mobile robot, Proteus, navigates using advanced sensors and AI. It picks up and carries containers to the packing and shipping area, and knows when to zip back to a charging point for a power-up.

On-board computer helps with fleet management and warehouse management.

Cameras are both upward and downward facing and can read barcodes.

Coloured lights are LEDs (Light Emitting Diodes).

Lidar for navigation and manoeuvring underneath carts.

Motors to drive wheels and as a powerlifting mechanism.

For safety, the robots' operating area is often **separate** from the human work area.

Hercules and Titan
These wheeled, flat-topped robots pick up heavy items. There's a marked grid on the floor to help them find their way around.

Hercules is fitted with a 3D camera to identify people and objects in its path.

Titan robot may look small, but it can carry huge, bulky items across the floor.

Sparrow
This robot arm picks up and sorts customer packages before shipment.

Robot technician
I used to work in the warehouse collecting and packing products. When they introduced robots, I retrained to look after them. I clean their wheels, cameras, and sensors, and check the batteries are recharging.

Shopping with robots

Some larger stores, such as Walmart in the USA, use lots of different types of robots. They keep busy scanning shelves, adding prices and labels, and keeping everything clean. Some robots are super friendly and greet customers as they walk into the store.

Auto-S
The tall Auto-S robot moves down the aisle scanning the shelves for out-of-stock products, incorrect prices, and missing labels. It sends an alert which prompts the restocking system to supply more products to the shelves.

Auto-C
A floor-scrubber robot, called Auto-C, works day and night. It follows a mapped route around the store, cleaning the floor as it goes.

In-store helper robots
Meet Peppa from Softbank Robotics, Japan. She's a human-like helper robot who moves on wheels, waves her arms, and talks. She welcomes customers, answers questions, recommends products, and helps people find what they are looking for in the store.

Stock manager

Robots check stock and move products much quicker than people and make fewer mistakes. When there is an empty space on the shelf, the store loses a sale, and the consumers are disappointed. Robots are expensive to install in the short term, but long term, they improve sales and provide good service.

Store manager

In-store helper robots show product promotions on their screen and guide customers to the products they want to find. The robot collects data about customers' shopping habits, which helps us decide which products to stock, the layout of the store, and if our price promotions and special offers are appealing.

Robot courier

We're trialling autonomous delivery robots, which can deliver packages to your door. These mini-vehicles roll along the pavement, cross roads, and avoid pedestrians to reach an address. The customer can unlock the compartment containing their package with a code sent to the app on a phone.

In the UK and USA, around **half of consumers shop online** and want fast, direct delivery to their homes.

Drone delivery

Flying drones can carry and drop a parcel to your doorstep. Like self-drive cars, they use sensors and software, such as GPS. However, drones operate in airspace, so also rely on altitude sensors to fly over obstacles like buildings and trees.

Artificial intelligence

How does a computer gain intelligence?
There are several ways in which computers can be said to gather intelligence. The Internet of Things (IoT) is the network of smart devices, vehicles, appliances, and other objects that feature sensors, along with software and network connectivity, allowing them to collect and share data with other devices. They collectively create a bank of knowledge and information from which AI devices learn.

Artificial intelligence

AI is short for artificial intelligence. It's a field of computer science that aims to perform tasks that usually require human intelligence. AI software runs on a computer. It can process information, solve problems, learn patterns, make decisions, and adapt to new situations. While it can be compared to a human brain, it thinks and learns in a different way.

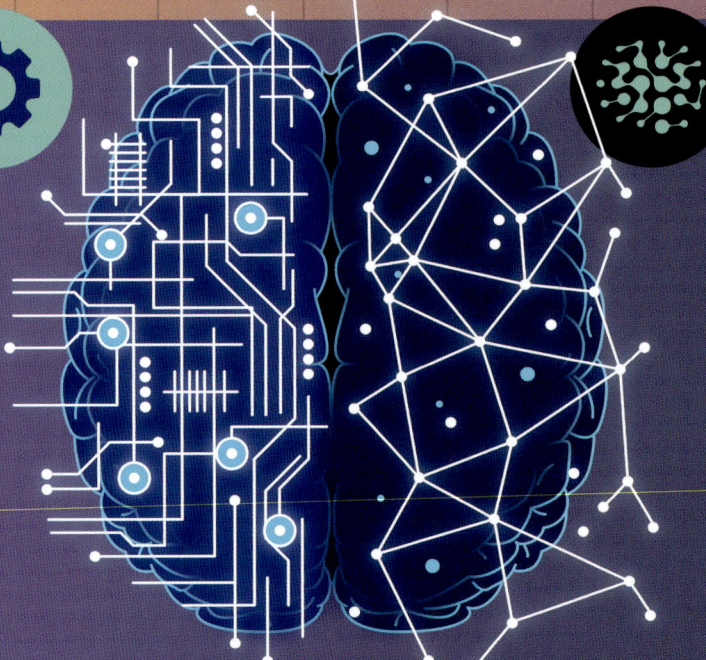

Machine learning
AI can "learn" by following rules, called algorithms. It can be compared to following a recipe. We may try out a recipe several times and improve it. In a similar way, a computer can test an algorithm rapidly a million times. It will need some human input to add more instructions where needed (the coding of the algorithms) but it will soon create a perfect result.

Deep learning
A subset of machine learning, in deep learning, data is processed using a model called a neural network, which has multiple layers and connections. It enables the processing of complex data and decision-making and can react to sudden changes in information instantly. The safety of self-drive vehicles relies on deep learning.

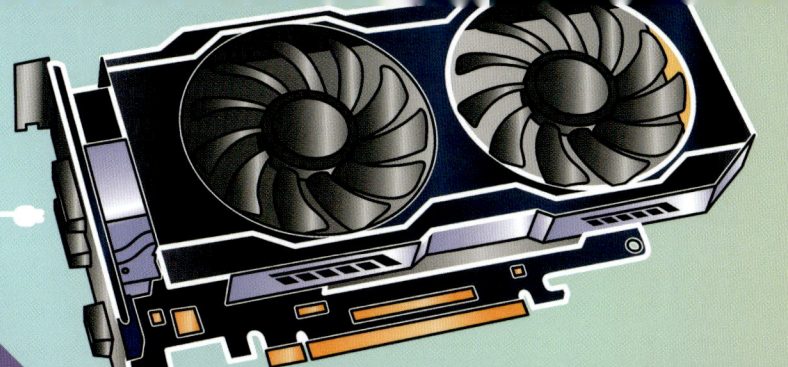

Graphical Processing Unit (GPU)
A GPU computes intensive tasks and multitasks at speed. It creates and handles images, gaming graphics, animations, and videos.

Natural Language Processing (NLP)
This enables computers and digital devices to recognize, understand, and generate written language and speech. NLP is used in chatbots and digital assistants such as Siri, Alexa, Google, and Cortana.

Computer vision
This trains computers to take meaningful information from digital images and videos, identify and classify objects, and react to what they see. Examples include facial recognition and self-driving cars.

The age of Big Data
We are living in the age of "Big Data". Data is information that shows human behaviour and product and service usage. It's stored on the internet or on an organization's network. Today, it's impossible to keep track of the enormous amounts of data created and shared every day in the world. Only some data is useful. We need intelligent, rapid computing to help us sort through it all. AI quickly processes masses of data, and programmers can instruct it to search for specific data types or patterns.

Every time we log-on to the internet, use a service, buy a product, or travel from one place to another, we create data.

Vertical farming

Vertical farming

Growing enough food for the world's population is a constant challenge. Many of the tasks required to grow and harvest food are repetitive and time-consuming – perfect work for robots. A method of growing crops indoors, called vertical farming, uses robots to grow more crops.

Robot harvester
Robots can detect weeds, spray chemicals, and move fruit and vegetables onto a conveyor before transporting them to a crate for packing.

What are vertical farms?
Vertical farms grow food crops in containers stacked like shelves. The plants grow in a greenhouse or an indoor space with artificial sun lamps, and the environment is controlled and monitored. So vertical farms could exist anywhere, even in the Arctic! These farms produce much more food using less land and water, and robots are proving useful assistants.

How they started
In 1999, Professor Dickson Despommier at Columbia University, USA, designed – together with his students – a skyscraper farm that could feed 50,000 people. This inspired the idea of vertical farming, allowing food to be grown indoors near customers and enabling countries to grow crops more easily.

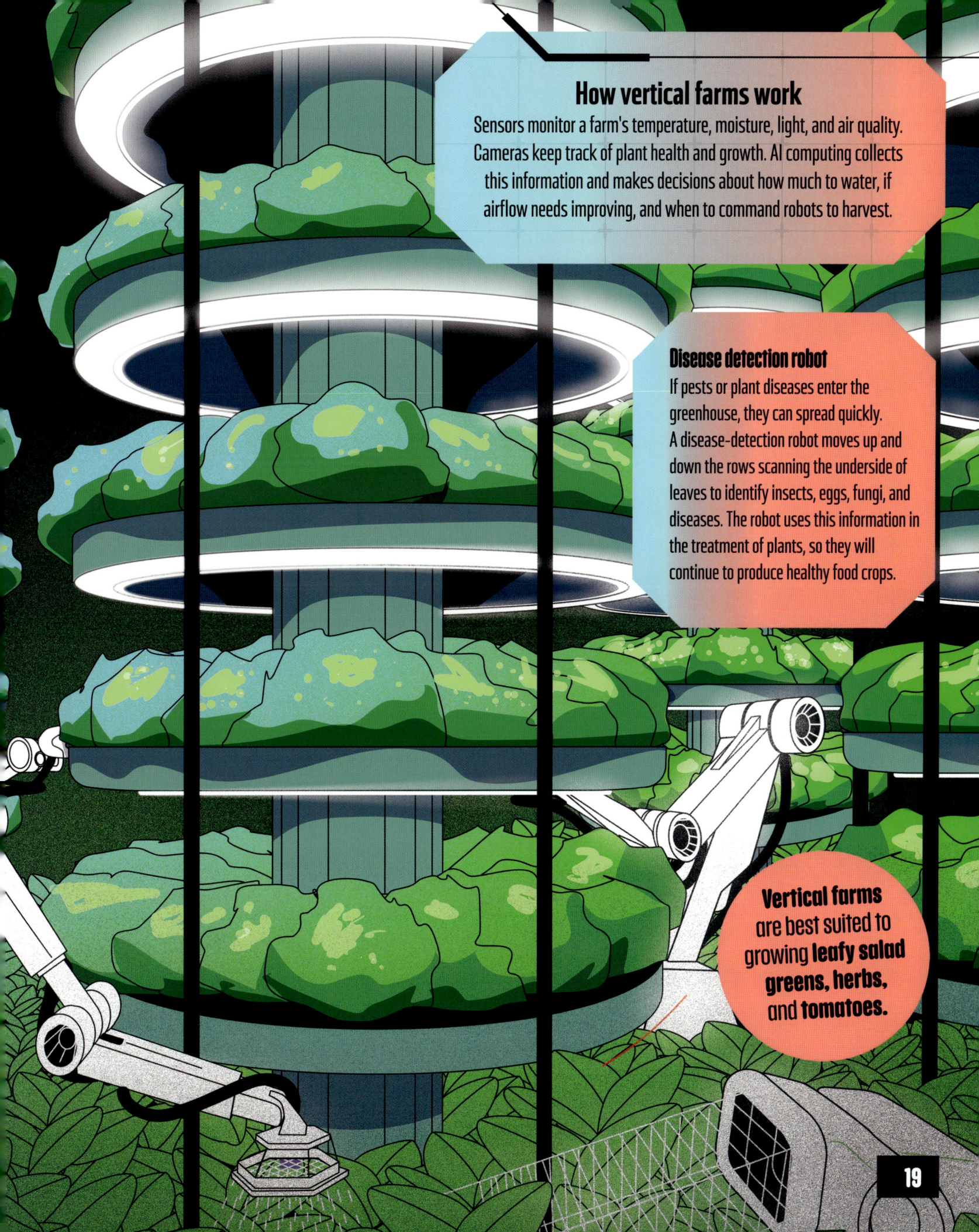

How vertical farms work
Sensors monitor a farm's temperature, moisture, light, and air quality. Cameras keep track of plant health and growth. AI computing collects this information and makes decisions about how much to water, if airflow needs improving, and when to command robots to harvest.

Disease detection robot
If pests or plant diseases enter the greenhouse, they can spread quickly. A disease-detection robot moves up and down the rows scanning the underside of leaves to identify insects, eggs, fungi, and diseases. The robot uses this information in the treatment of plants, so they will continue to produce healthy food crops.

Vertical farms are best suited to growing **leafy salad greens, herbs,** and **tomatoes.**

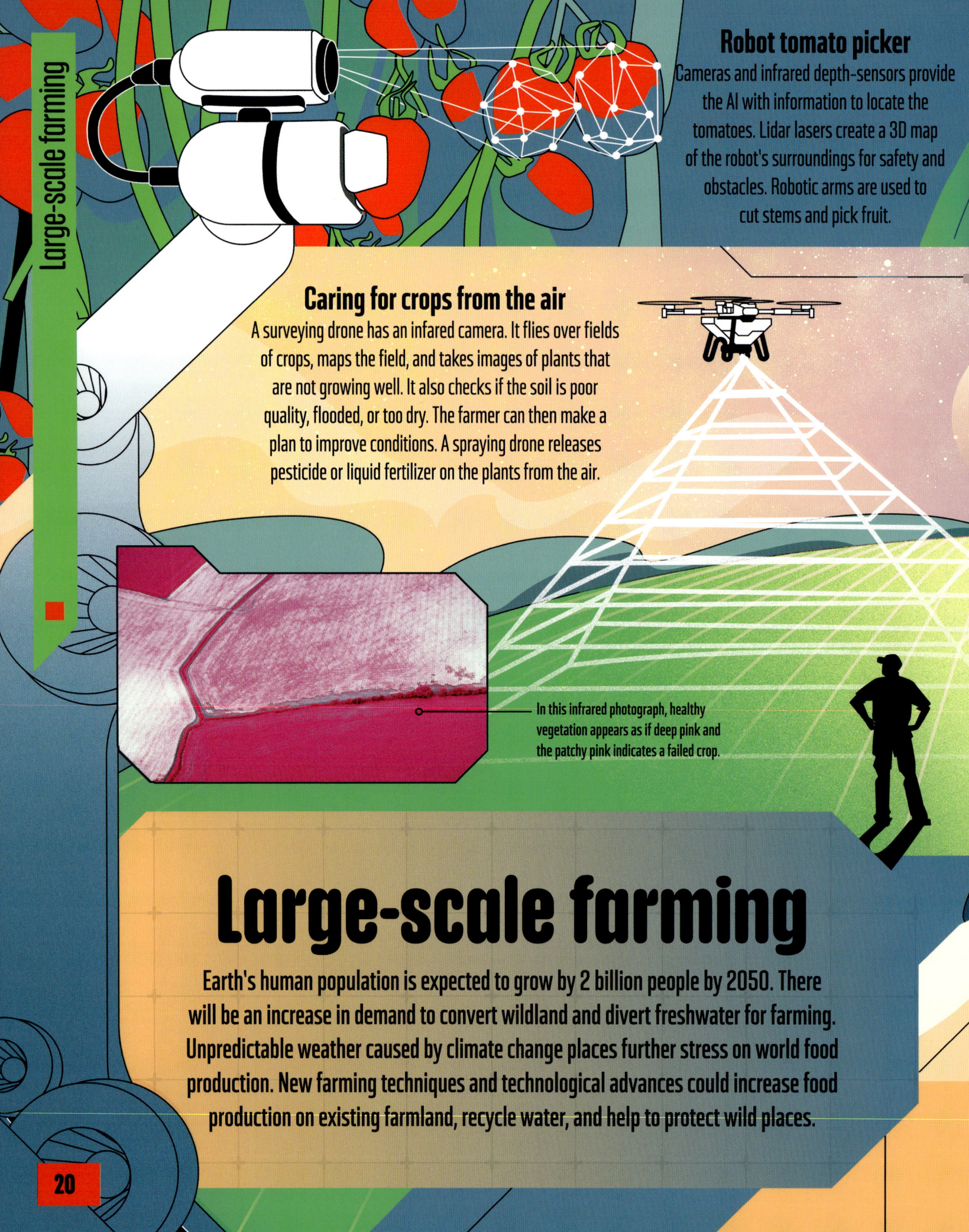

Large-scale farming

Robot tomato picker
Cameras and infrared depth-sensors provide the AI with information to locate the tomatoes. Lidar lasers create a 3D map of the robot's surroundings for safety and obstacles. Robotic arms are used to cut stems and pick fruit.

Caring for crops from the air
A surveying drone has an infared camera. It flies over fields of crops, maps the field, and takes images of plants that are not growing well. It also checks if the soil is poor quality, flooded, or too dry. The farmer can then make a plan to improve conditions. A spraying drone releases pesticide or liquid fertilizer on the plants from the air.

In this infrared photograph, healthy vegetation appears as if deep pink and the patchy pink indicates a failed crop.

Large-scale farming

Earth's human population is expected to grow by 2 billion people by 2050. There will be an increase in demand to convert wildland and divert freshwater for farming. Unpredictable weather caused by climate change places further stress on world food production. New farming techniques and technological advances could increase food production on existing farmland, recycle water, and help to protect wild places.

The use of computerized drones in farming mean that **farm workers no longer have to handle dangerous chemicals.**

Self-drive tractors
An autonomous tractor might work day and night in a field, and farmers can hook-up existing farm equipment – such as a sprayer, plough, or harvester.

Picking-arm
A picking-arm for apples uses both grip and suction to pull the fruit from the branch and place it onto a conveyor. If the grip or suction is too strong, it will bruise the fruit; too weak and the fruit will fall to the ground. Sensors and cameras locate the fruit, and the robot adjusts the pressure required for the size and shape of each apple.

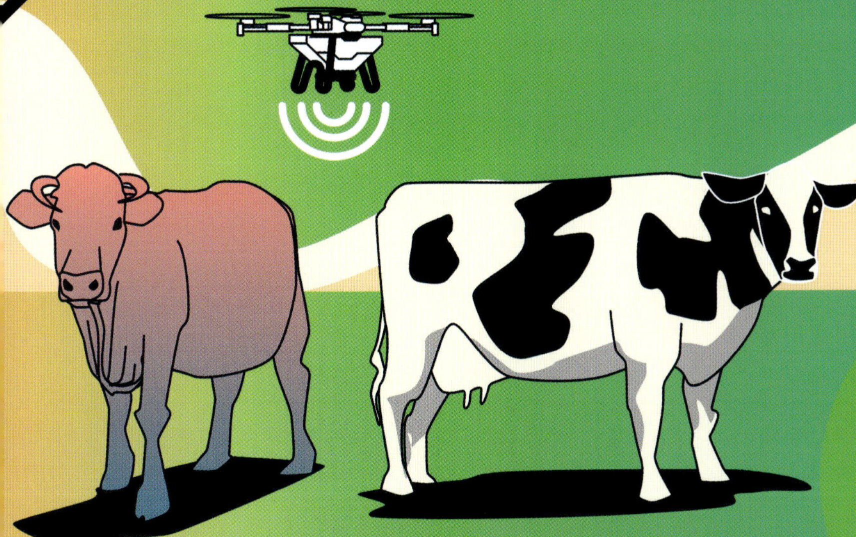

Cattle farmer
The herd grazes over a vast wild area. There are no roads and tracking them down from an off-road vehicle or on horseback takes time. With a drone, we can follow their trail from the air, find and count them, and check for stray or sick animals.

Smart farming

Harvesting and picking crops can be repetitive, and it also needs a careful touch. Agricultural robots are designed so that they don't harm the fruit or vegetables as they pick them. **This picture shows what smart farming could be like in the future! This robot is picking up lettuce**, and the autonomous vehicle transports the leafy greens away.

Making motor vehicles

Many of the products we use every day, such as a toaster, a car, or a pen, are made in factories. Workers assemble the product step-by-step, adding different materials and parts. This is called a production or assembly line. Most tasks on an assembly line are highly repetitive, making them ideal work for robots. The automotive (cars, lorries, and motorbikes) industry is the largest user of robots in the world.

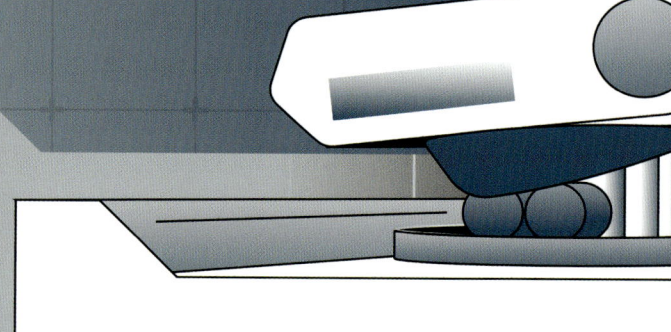

First industrial robot

In 1961, people introduced the first industrial robot, which they named Unimate. It was a robotic arm secured to the floor, powered by electric motors and hydraulic actuators. Unimate could swivel around, move up and down, and pick things up with its gripper hand. Car-makers used the robot to move metal parts to moulding (shaping) or welding (joining together) workstations. Today, industrial robots vary in size, automation, and autonomy. They use many tools, but the fixed strong-arm is still a common design.

Making vehicles

Robot arms are positioned along the assembly line to handle the many materials and techniques needed to assemble vehicles. Robots make production safer and more efficient, resulting in better-quality vehicles. Let's meet these powerful robots...

Cartesian

These pickup-and-place robots can only move their arm in a straight line up and down, forward and back, and left and right. They lift heavy motors and fuel systems into place in the vehicle.

Articulated

These heavy-lifting robotic arms swivel in any direction and have multiple articulated (hinged) joints to pivot and grab objects. They weld, drill holes, insert windscreens, attach doors and bumpers, sand, paint, and polish vehicles.

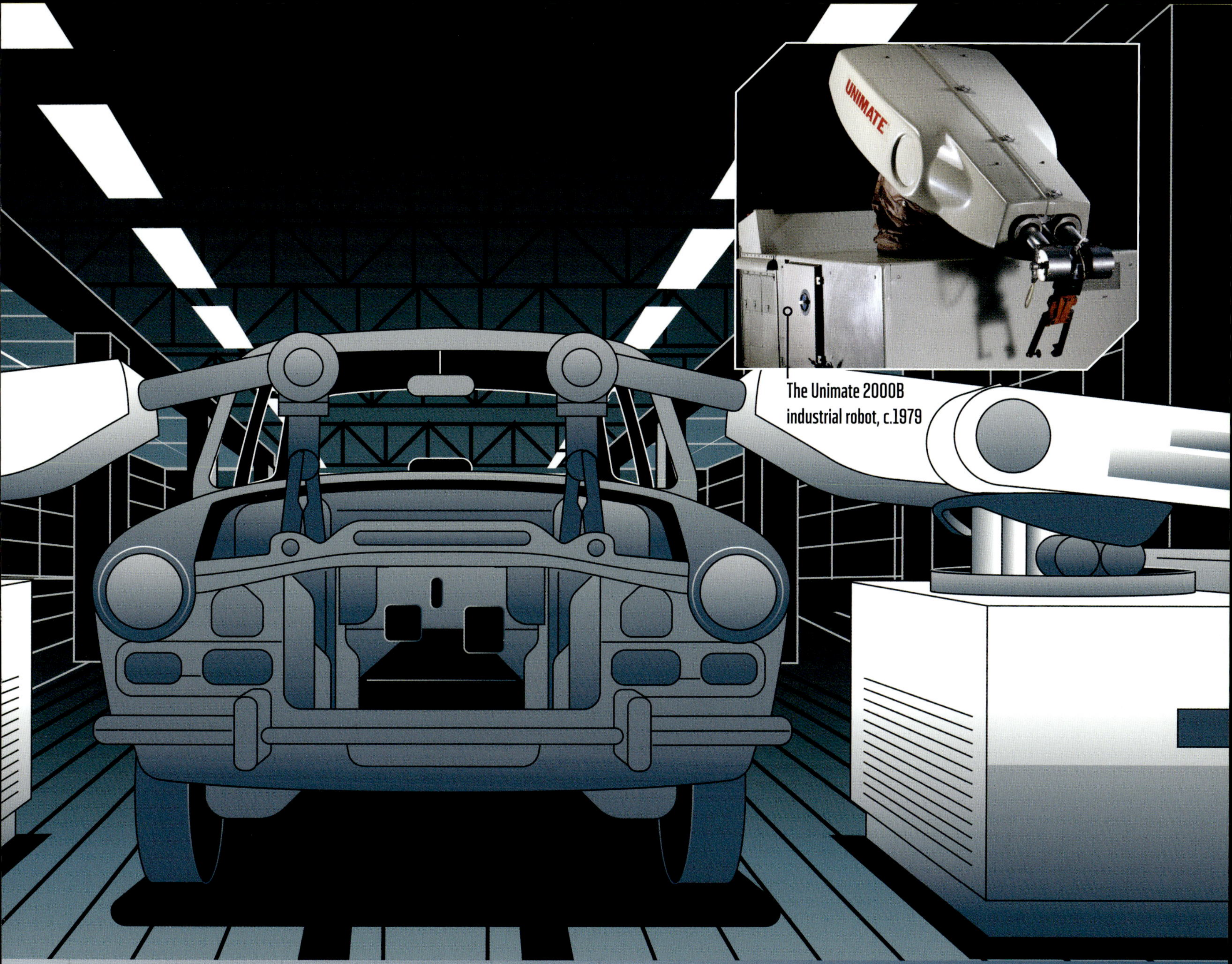

The Unimate 2000B industrial robot, c.1979

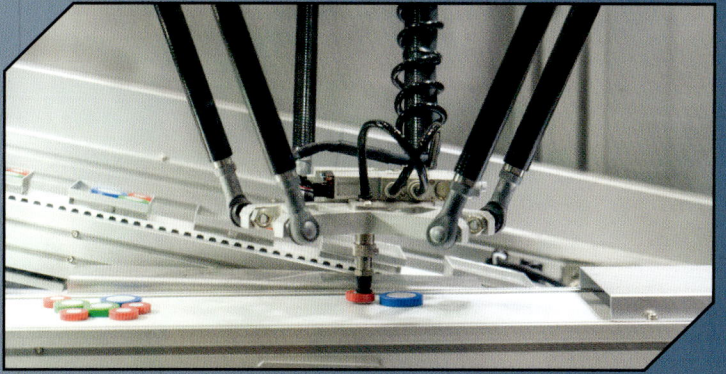

SCARA
This type of robot has very precise movements. It carries out detailed small-part assembly, such as building electronic circuit boards and cutting fabric for car interiors.

Delta
For smaller parts, these high-speed robotic arms are perfect. They assemble electronics such as pumps and motors and move the finished product onto a conveyor belt.

Working with people

In a car factory, it's too dangerous for human workers to be in the same area as fast-moving industrial robots. Cobots – or collaborative robots – are designed to work safely alongside humans in a shared workspace.

How cobots work

If a person gets too close, a cobot has safety mechanisms – such as force sensors, vision systems, and proximity sensors – that stop or slow it down. Cobots use different tools to perform repetitive tasks, such as inspections, labelling, picking up and moving small parts, and even turning screws and gluing things together. This frees up human workers to plan and problem-solve.

Car designer

Increasingly, car buyers like to choose the colour and parts of their new car, called customization. It makes our work challenging, as we need to use more parts and retool the production line to place these custom parts in the vehicle. This slows production down and increases costs. Cobots help us to do these changeover tasks efficiently and I can then design more customized colours and gadgets to please customers.

Figure 2

A humanoid robot called Figure 2 successfully loaded parts into a machine at a BMW vehicle factory as a test. Figure 2 understands voice commands and has natural speech. Six cameras sense surroundings, avoid obstacles, and enable hand-eye coordination to identify and pick up items. The robot has a human-like wrist and hand with four fingers and a thumb to manipulate objects and do precise tasks only humans could previously do.

As humanoids become more advanced, they will outperform human workers. Robots can work day and night, be more consistent and precise, and can adapt to new tasks quickly.

Will factory workers be replaced?

There is a worldwide shortage of labour (human workers), and companies are looking to robots to solve this problem. While automation may replace many factory jobs, people will still be needed for roles that require engineering, decision-making, and problem-solving skills.

How do robots sense?

Our five senses – sight, hearing, touch, smell, and taste – give us the power to understand and explore the world around us and observe changes. Robots are fitted with devices called sensors – these are like the robot's eyes, ears, hands, nose, and tongue. They collect information about the environment, enabling the robot to use this data to make decisions and perform tasks on their own.

Hearing
A microphone captures sounds and a robot's programming recognizes the sound and reacts. Speech recognition assistants such as Siri respond to voice commands.

Ultrasonic sensors
Some robots use ultrasonic sensors to "see" how far away things are. They work like a bat's echolocation. The robot sends out sound waves that bounce off objects, and by measuring how long it takes for the sound to return, the robot can tell how far away an object is.

What is proprioception?
Proprioception is the brain's ability to know where our body is in space and how it is moving. Our brains gather information from our senses to orientate, balance, and move smoothly. Robots use a gyroscope – a device that tells the robot which way up it is. An accelerometer tells the robot how fast it's going and pressure sensors relay the force required to touch or walk on different surfaces.

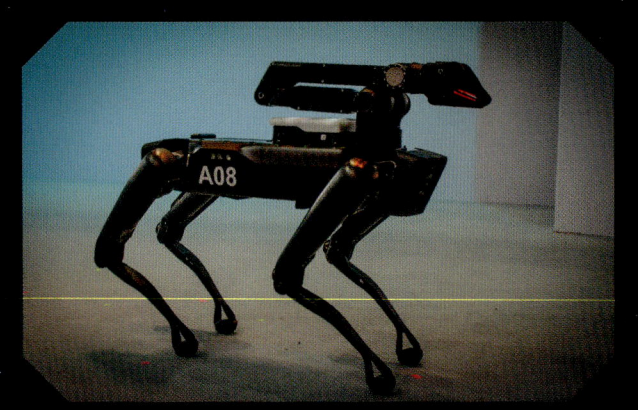

Touch
Pressure and tactile sensors are like robot "hands" and help the robot feel things. If the robot touches something, these sensors can tell if it's soft, hard, rough, smooth, hot, or cold. Touch sensors and cameras often work together to enable a robot to understand shapes and handle complex or delicate objects, such as ripe fruit.

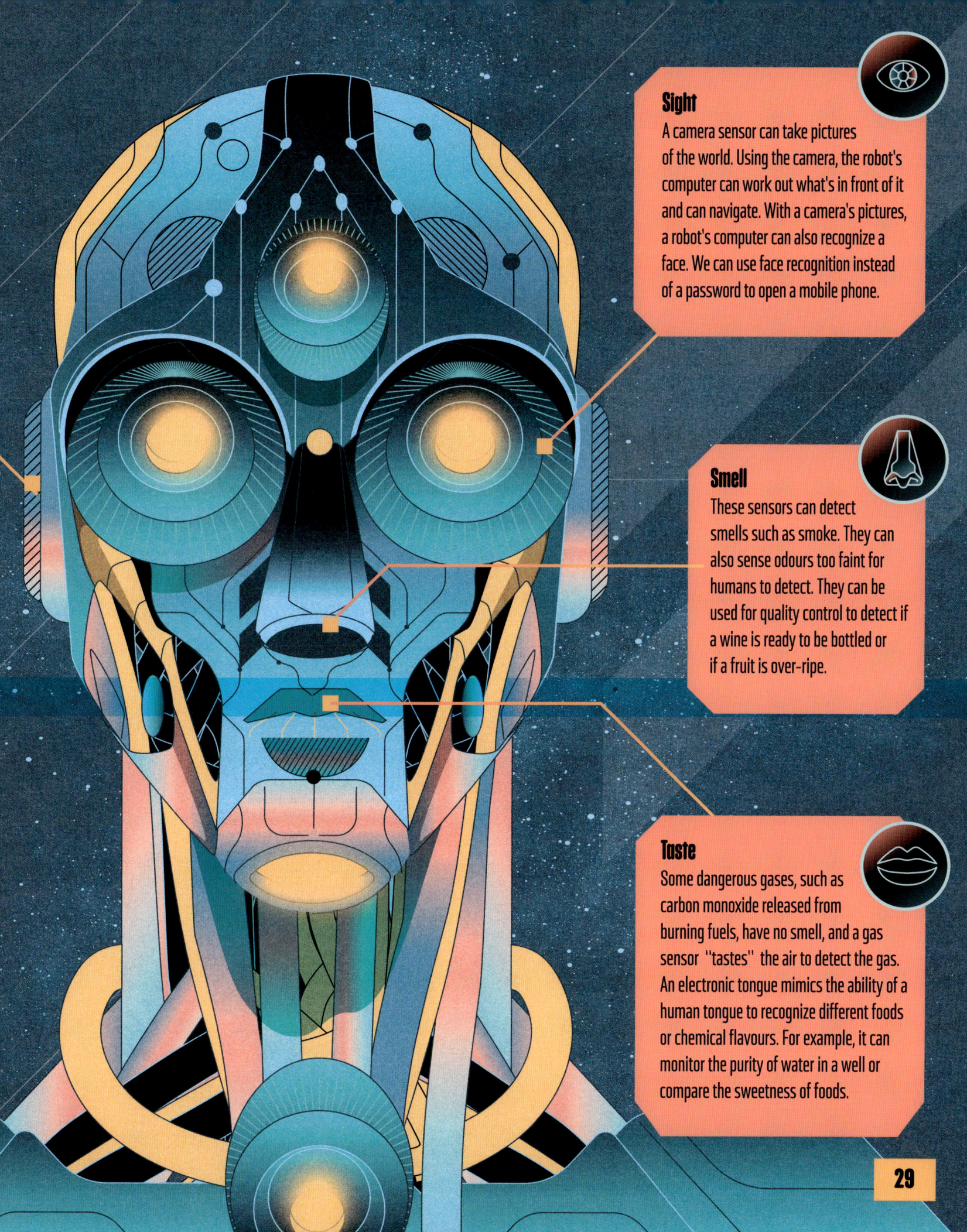

Sight
A camera sensor can take pictures of the world. Using the camera, the robot's computer can work out what's in front of it and can navigate. With a camera's pictures, a robot's computer can also recognize a face. We can use face recognition instead of a password to open a mobile phone.

Smell
These sensors can detect smells such as smoke. They can also sense odours too faint for humans to detect. They can be used for quality control to detect if a wine is ready to be bottled or if a fruit is over-ripe.

Taste
Some dangerous gases, such as carbon monoxide released from burning fuels, have no smell, and a gas sensor "tastes" the air to detect the gas. An electronic tongue mimics the ability of a human tongue to recognize different foods or chemical flavours. For example, it can monitor the purity of water in a well or compare the sweetness of foods.

Medical robots

Helping to improve healthcare and save lives, medical robots work alongside surgeons in the operating theatre, offer new treatments to cancer patients, improve the mobility and lives of disabled people, and help to clean and organize hospitals.

The Da Vinci robot

Surgeons have safely performed over 14 million surgeries with the Da Vinci robot. The robot has four arms that hold tiny surgical instruments. First, the surgeon makes small cuts through which he inserts the robot's tiny camera and tools. Then the surgeon controls the robot from a nearby console with hand and foot controls and a screen. The surgeon can zoom in up to 10 times to see an enlarged picture of the insides of the patient's body.

Boom arm swings the robot into position over the patient.

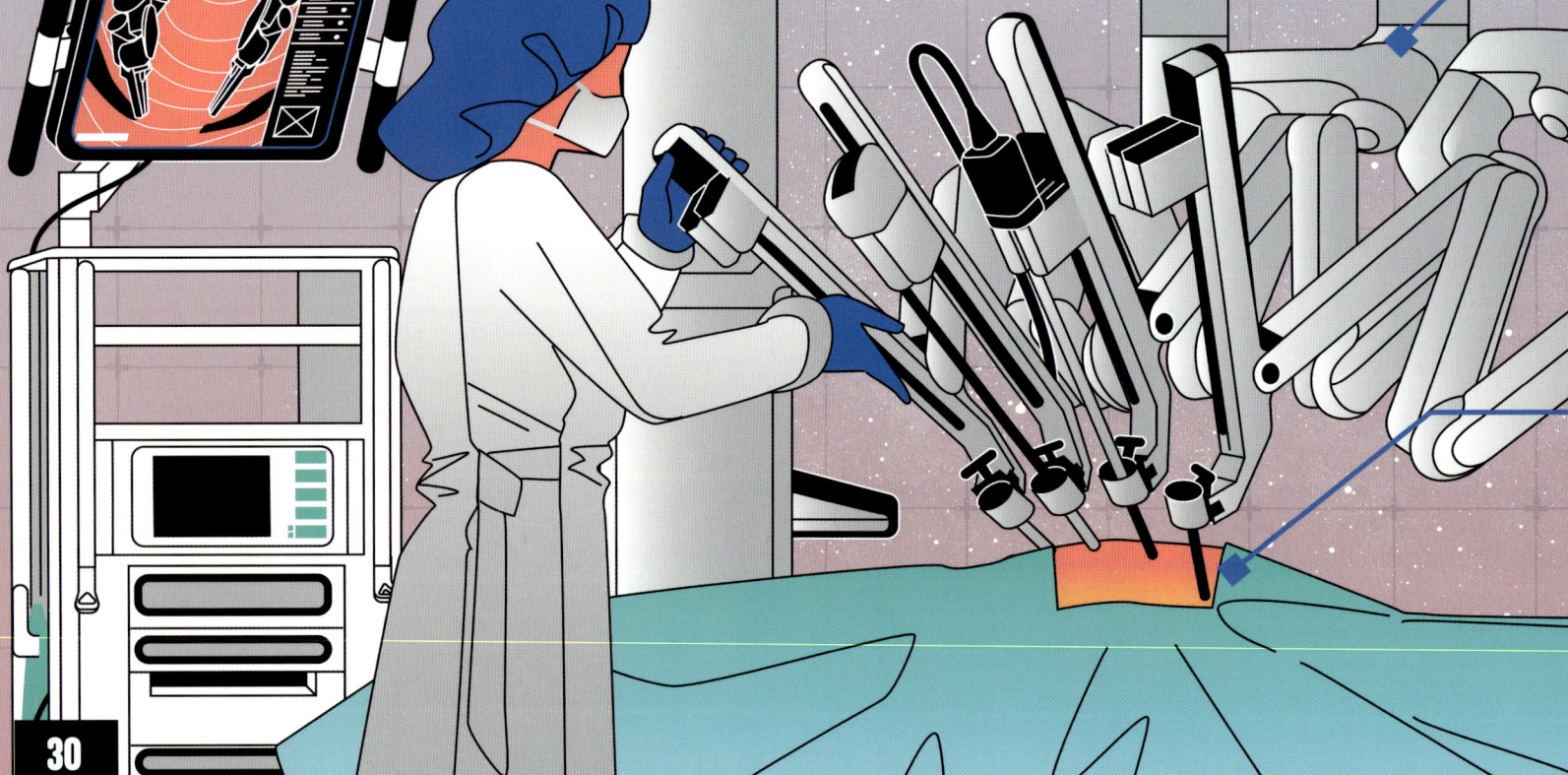

Motor-powered joints allow for a wide range of movement to perform surgery safely.

Articulated joints on the robotic arms follow the surgeon's movements with great precision.

3D cameras are fitted on the robot, which help the surgeon see what they are doing.

Surgical tools are attached to the rods at the end of each arm.

Cyberknife

This large robotic arm is used to treat cancer cells in the body. The robot emits a high-energy beam of light that passes through the skin to target the cells. Images taken during the treatment check the progress. Radiation kills the cells or slows their growth. The robot arm circles the patient, and the joints bend to deliver radiation doses with precision to the part of the body that needs treatment. The robot has sensors that can detect coughing or breathing and adjust the radiation beam to keep it on target, so healthy cells aren't accidentally damaged.

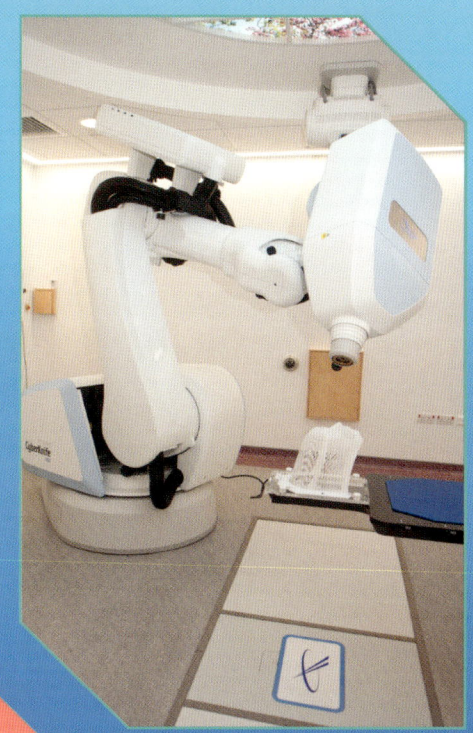

Hospital-helper robots

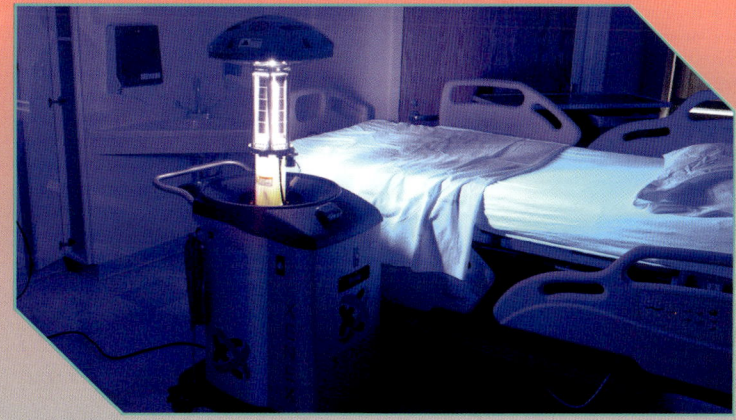

Xenex (USA) keeps hospitals clean by beaming UV rays of light in all directions around a room. UV light kills tough germs that can infect patients and make them sicker.

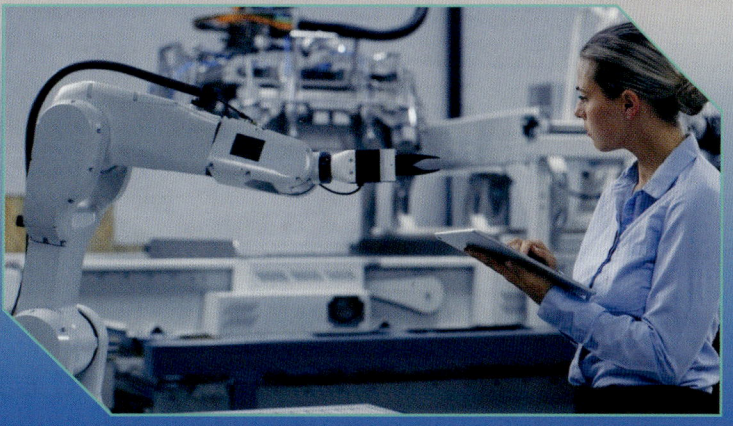

The Tug made by Aethon, USA, uses driverless vehicle technology to travel autonomously around the hospital, delivering meals, bedding, and medicines.

Bionic humans

Some people are born without limbs, or an illness or injury can lead to the loss of movement and mobility to the spine, legs, or arms. Bionic technology improves independence and quality of life for people with disabilities and can help them get back on their feet. Human bionic engineers combine knowledge of biological sciences and technology to design and build devices that mimic or improve the form and movement of the human body.

Exoskeletons

An exoskeleton is a bionic suit worn on the outside of the body. Motors, sensors, and mechanical parts help to move the legs, back, or arms of the disabled person and support muscles and joints. A person who has lost the use of their legs can stand, balance, walk, and sit down again while wearing the exoskeleton. Over time, it helps the body get stronger, and if possible, re-teaches the brain and muscles to walk again.

EksoNR, Eksobionics (USA)

EksoNR has a lightweight frame and attaches to the body with supports and straps. Sensors include a gyroscope, which is an instrument that tracks posture and balance, and an accelerometer, which detects motion, and together they help keep the wearer stable. Sensors feel when a person wants to move. The motors act like muscles, helping the legs to move by making them bend, step forward, or stand straight.

The computer
captures information about the patient's movements so doctors can adjust the movement and speed to suit a patient's ability and progress.

Sensors
send information to the control computer, which activates the motors in the joints.

Safety first

Workers can suffer neck and back pain caused by muscle strain from doing repetitive tasks, lifting heavy objects, and poor body posture. An exoskeleton correctly aligns the body and assists muscle movement, helping prevent injuries, and reducing strain and improving posture for all workers.

Neural interfaces

This innovative technology allows people to control machines with their thoughts. A device equipped with sensors is placed on the head and linked to the brain. A person with paralysis might use a neural interface to move a robotic arm or operate a wheelchair simply by thinking about the movement. In the future, neural brain interfaces could restore lost senses and improve damaged brain function.

Bionic arm

A type of prosthetic (artificial) limb, the bionic arm has advanced technology to mimic the strength and movements of a natural arm. To attach the limb, technicians position sensors on the person's upper arm. When the person tries to move, sensors pick up signals from their muscles, and the arm's computer uses these signals to move the robotic joints.

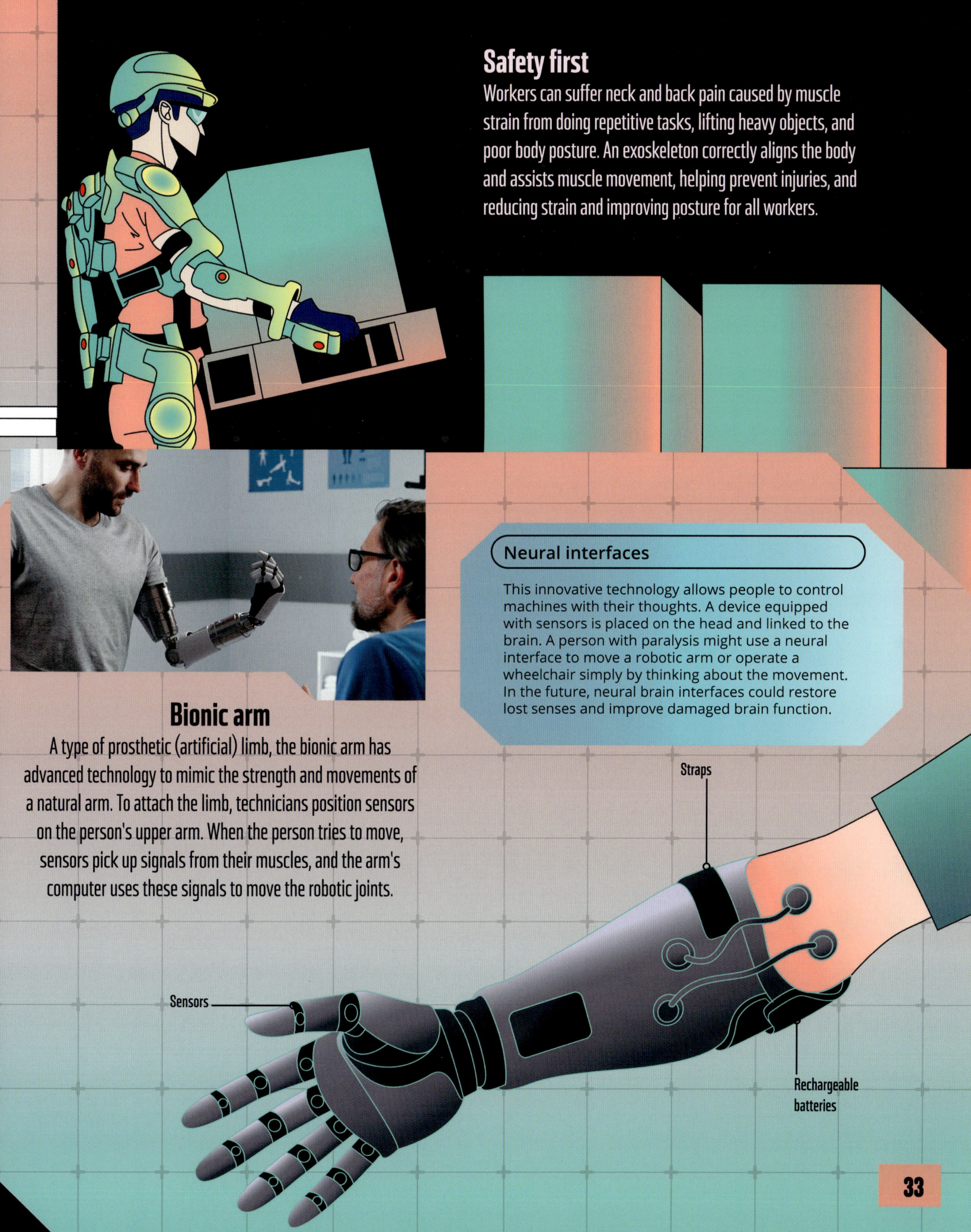

Straps

Rechargeable batteries

Sensors

Helpers at home

Say goodbye to chores! Robots are arriving in the home to help us with boring everyday tasks so we can spend more time learning, playing, and relaxing.

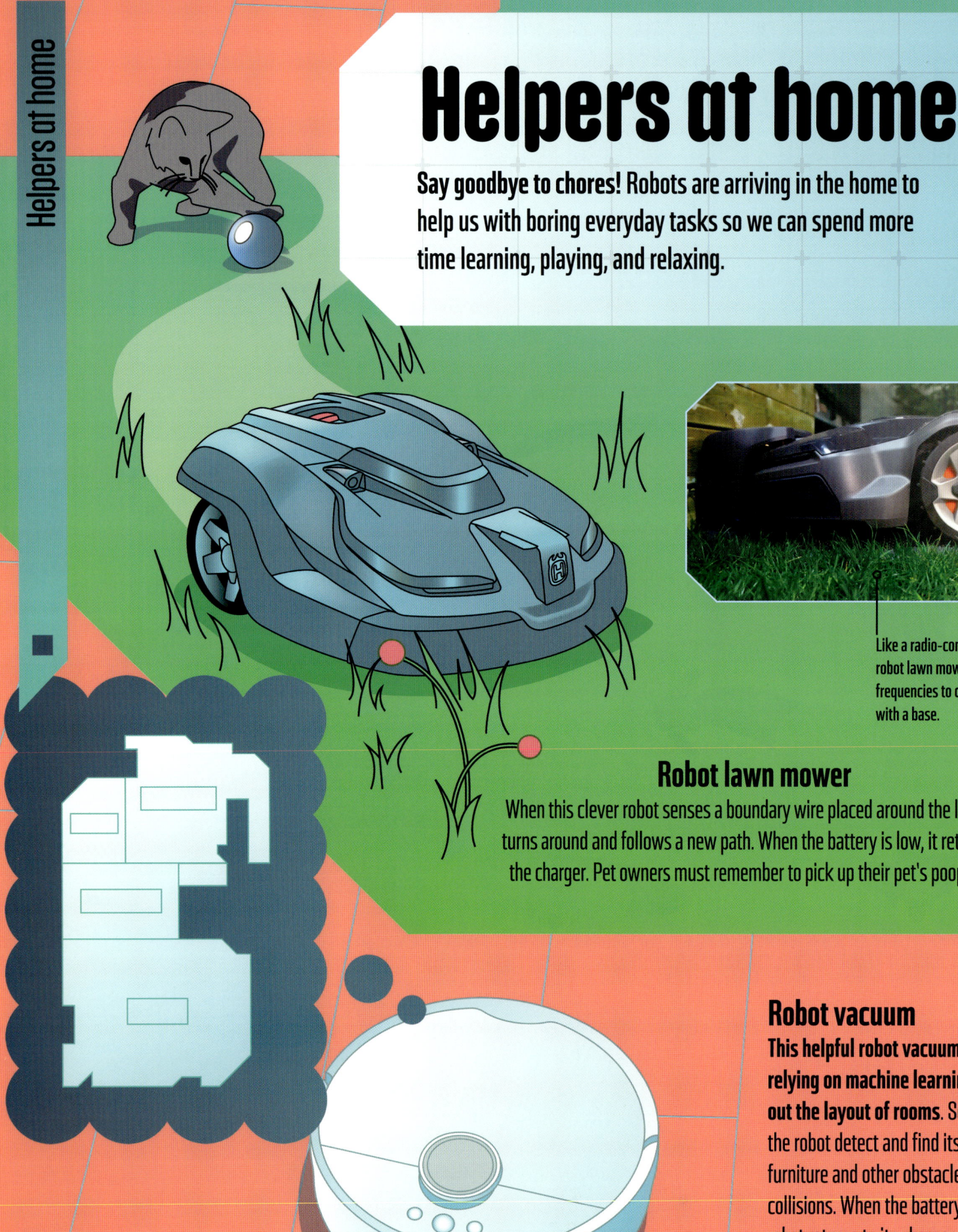

Like a radio-controlled car, robot lawn mowers use radio frequencies to communicate with a base.

Robot lawn mower
When this clever robot senses a boundary wire placed around the lawn, it turns around and follows a new path. When the battery is low, it returns to the charger. Pet owners must remember to pick up their pet's poop first!

Robot vacuum
This helpful robot vacuums the floor, relying on machine learning to work out the layout of rooms. Sensors help the robot detect and find its way around furniture and other obstacles, preventing collisions. When the battery is low, the robot returns to its charger.

Robot window-cleaner

If you look up at tall buildings in a city, there's a good chance you'll see a window-cleaning bot at work. The bot works on any window, using vacuum suction to stick to the glass. It measures the size of the window with a laser beam, then sprays cleaning solution. Cloth pads wipe the window as it moves along on tracks, and there's a safety cord if power fails and it falls.

Hi. I have voice recognition software, so I know who you are, and you can ask me direct questions. My AI enables me to become smarter over time through software updates, accessing the internet, and by your requests. I'll also learn your preferences and habits and adapt to changes.

Virtual AI assistants

In 2011, Apple launched Siri, the first virtual assistant. Users say "Siri" to activate the assistant on an Apple smart device. Siri understands and responds to verbal or written questions and requests, such as "Play my rock music playlist". Today there are several AI assistants available, which also connect to other smart devices in the home to program heating, turn on the lights, activate security systems, set reminders, and much more!

Clever robots!

Humanoid AI robot helpers are here! The field of humanoid AI robotics is rapidly evolving. Roboticists are placing advanced AI technology in the "brains" of humanoid robots to make the ultimate home, work, or school smart assistant that can communicate, think, and move much like a human.

Optimus-Gen2

This robot assistant was launched by Tesla, USA, in 2024. It's designed to do repetitive, dangerous or boring tasks. The robot can autonomously walk, climb stairs, lift and carry objects, adjust to new situations, and make decisions.

Learn football with a robot friend!

Unitree G1 was developed in China and uses advanced AI. The robot moves fast after the ball, runs like a human, and doesn't mind being bumped into and knocked over. It has fully flexible hands so it can even carry your bag.

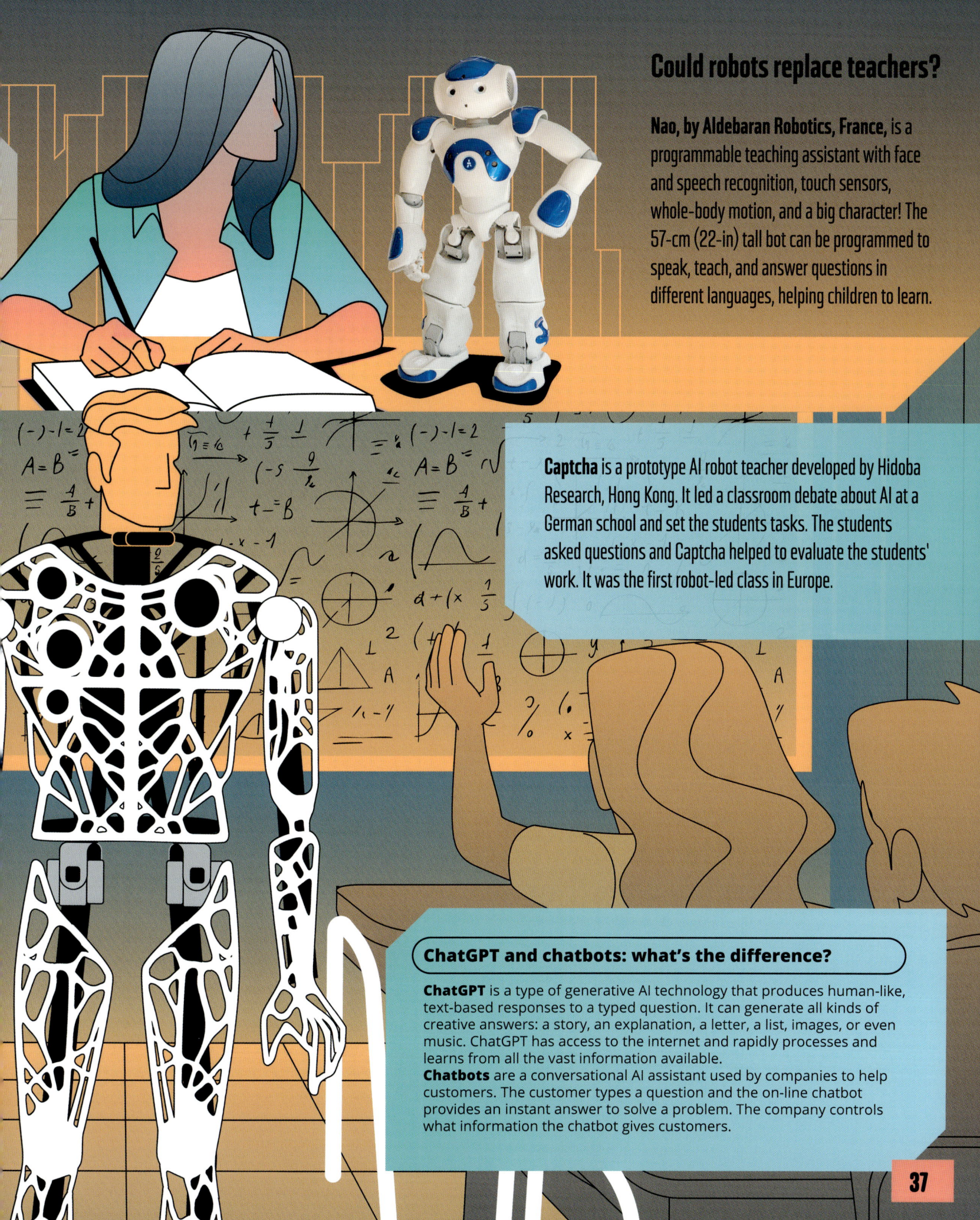

Could robots replace teachers?

Nao, by Aldebaran Robotics, France, is a programmable teaching assistant with face and speech recognition, touch sensors, whole-body motion, and a big character! The 57-cm (22-in) tall bot can be programmed to speak, teach, and answer questions in different languages, helping children to learn.

Captcha is a prototype AI robot teacher developed by Hidoba Research, Hong Kong. It led a classroom debate about AI at a German school and set the students tasks. The students asked questions and Captcha helped to evaluate the students' work. It was the first robot-led class in Europe.

ChatGPT and chatbots: what's the difference?

ChatGPT is a type of generative AI technology that produces human-like, text-based responses to a typed question. It can generate all kinds of creative answers: a story, an explanation, a letter, a list, images, or even music. ChatGPT has access to the internet and rapidly processes and learns from all the vast information available.

Chatbots are a conversational AI assistant used by companies to help customers. The customer types a question and the on-line chatbot provides an instant answer to solve a problem. The company controls what information the chatbot gives customers.

Emo

This cute desktop pet from Living.AI, China, can self-explore your desk without falling off it! The robot has thousands of faces and movements showing moods and feelings, which help it interact with its owner in a natural way. The sensors and AI tech track sounds, recognize people and objects, and help Emo learn from its surroundings.

Pleo

This robot from Innvo Labs, China, acts like a pet dino. It explores, learns, makes cute noises, and munches on plastic leaves. It needs lots of petting and attention, teaching children how to care for a pet.

Aibo

Designed by Sony, Japan, Aibo is a puppy companion bot. It makes an emotional bond with its owners right from the start by offering a paw in friendship. Aibo scratches, wags its tail, runs when called, and loves playing and being petted. The bot's AI learns from interactions and adjusts its behaviour and expressions to match its owner's needs.

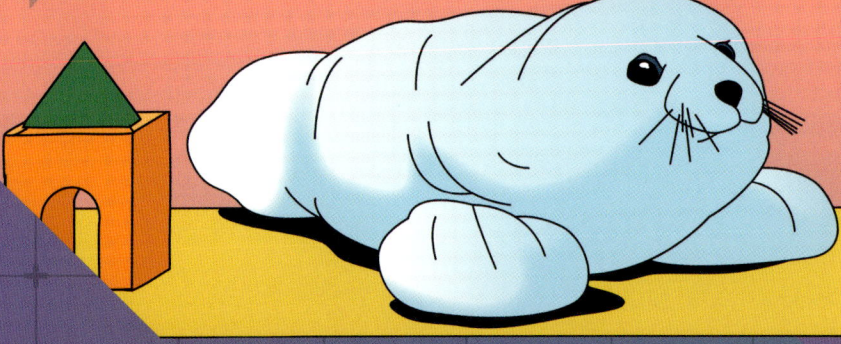

Paro

Meet Paro – a therapy robot seal that is used in hospitals and care homes. He's super-soft and people love to hug and talk to him. Paro relieves loneliness and stress, and brings comfort. For patients who've lost brain function because of illness, caring for a therapy bot can help to improve their memory, speech, and mobility.

Robotic toys

Robot companions are the friends that are always there! Expressions and movements are becoming increasingly lifelike, and AI tech means they can recognize and learn their owner's preferences. As well as being cute and great fun, they can be a learning tool and offer comfort if their owner is feeling lonely or anxious.

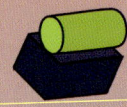

Click-bot

You can build and program Click-bot from KEYi Technology, China, yourself. It snaps together to make different shapes and fun characters. It has simple block-based coding that's easy for children to master on an app.

What is virtual reality (VR)?

When you put on a VR headset, often linked to a gaming console, you step into another world. Whether playing in a giant football stadium, swimming underwater in an alien world, or flying a spaceship – anything is possible. The VR headset makes you feel as if you are inside the game or part of the adventure. Handheld controls or haptic gloves vibrate, adding to the sense of reality.

RotoVR explorer

This gaming chair from Roto/Meta, UK, connects to a VR headset and automatically follows the player's head movement, turning the player around in the chair and providing a smooth, natural 360-degree circular view of the virtual world. Vibrations felt throughout the chair add to the immersive experience.

What is augmented reality (AR)?

Imagine looking at your phone screen with the camera pointed at the room and a teddy bear is walking around, or pointing the phone at your friend and on screen they're wearing a funny hat and glasses. AR apps make the real world more interactive and are a lot of fun.

Ocean conservation

Our oceans sustain us by producing rain, food, jobs, and medicine. They also inspire culture and sports, and are a place of discovery. Climate change and pollution are putting marine ecosystems under pressure. Scientists and engineers believe robotic technology can help clean up our oceans and protect sea life.

Oceans are not a rubbish bin!
Plastic arrives in our oceans in many ways. Rainwater and wind carry loose plastic into rivers, which flow to the sea. We flush plastics down the toilet, and sewage pumps carry it to the ocean. The amount of plastic in the sea is rapidly increasing, poisoning the food supply.

Jellyfish robot
This soft-tentacled robot could help with the plastic problem. Inspired by the moon jellyfish, the robot jellyfish moves through water, catching plastic with its tentacle grabbers and trapping rubbish under its body. The robot is designed to live among sea creatures on a fragile coral reef without disturbing the ecosystem. It swims independently, powered by batteries, or controlled via a wire tether.

Rechargeable batteries

Electrohydraulic actuators act like muscles, moving outwards and inwards to create buoyancy and movement.

6 tentacles with soft grabbers.

Robot engineer
Most ocean plastic ends up on the ocean floor where it's hard to retrieve. The jellyfish robot catches pollution before it sinks. We are developing the robot to work more autonomously and for longer, to travel over a wide area and in a group, and to be constructed from materials that will not harm the environment.

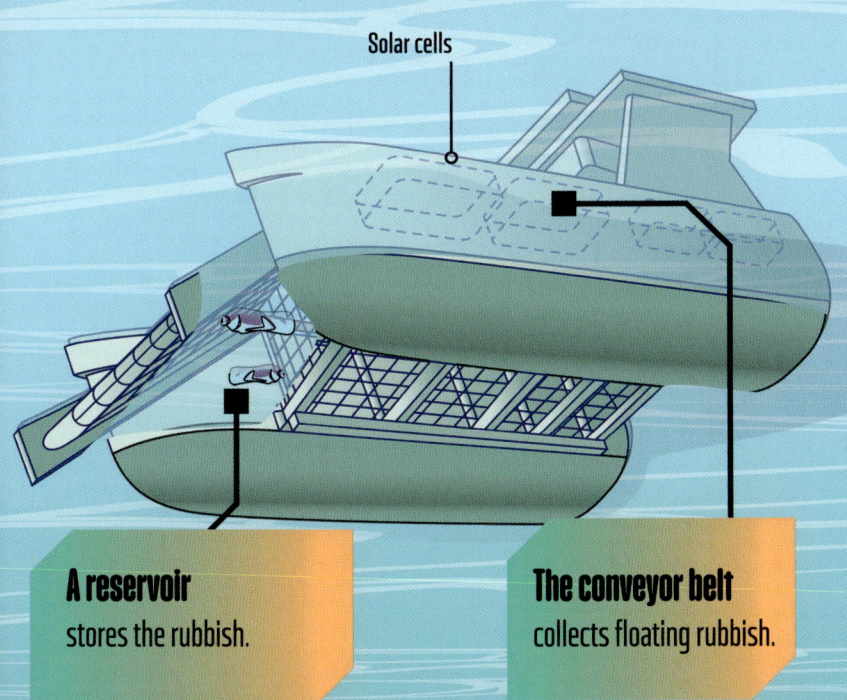

Solar cells

Clearbot
This autonomous boat scoops up and collects floating rubbish from polluted rivers and harbours. AI programming identifies the type and size of rubbish and enables the boat to work as part of a fleet.

A reservoir stores the rubbish.

The conveyor belt collects floating rubbish.

As designs and technology improves, robots are increasingly playing their part in protecting the world's oceans and seas.

Lavalboat
To help damaged coral reefs, scientists from the University of Hawaii, USA, collect coral spawn and place it in nursery tanks to grow. When the coral babies are big enough, a small robotic boat releases them into the water above a damaged reef. Each tiny coral, called a polyp, attaches to the seabed and forms a new, growing coral.

Propellors

Container is used for storing the larvae.

Tubes for releasing larvae.

Coral scientist
Once a year when there is a full moon and the sea temperature is just right, coral spawn, sending clouds of eggs into the water. The coral eggs grow into larvae that float on the currents and tides until big enough to sink to the seabed to grow. Most new corals do not survive. We want to increase their chances of survival and make sure that baby corals settle on damaged reefs to replenish them.

Land conservation

Aerial robots – such as satellites and flying drones – are already used to monitor deforestation, and to survey and track wild animals. Can robots also work on the ground to help restore habitats, protect Earth's amazing biodiversity, and even move among animals mimicking their behaviour?

Monitoring the planet
Seasonal weather and human activity all leave a mark on the Earth. Imaging satellites orbit the planet, recording these changes. Conservationists use satellite data to help track the movements of endangered animals such as tigers, elephants, and chimpanzees.

Conservationist
Using a live camera on the base of a drone, I can view and count the tree-nests of a troop of chimpanzees and track their seasonal movement through the forest to find food. I fly the drones at a distance to avoid frightening the animals.

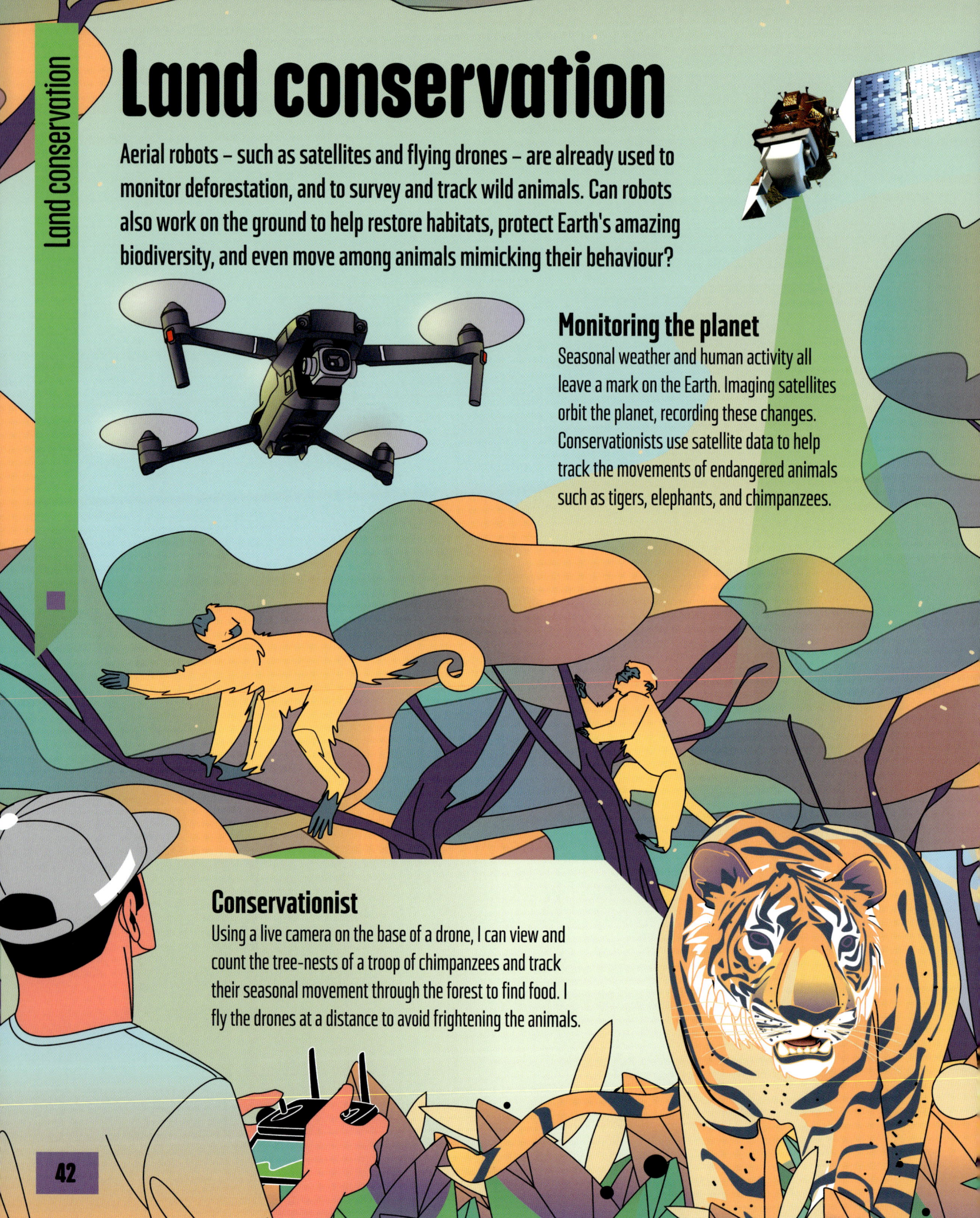

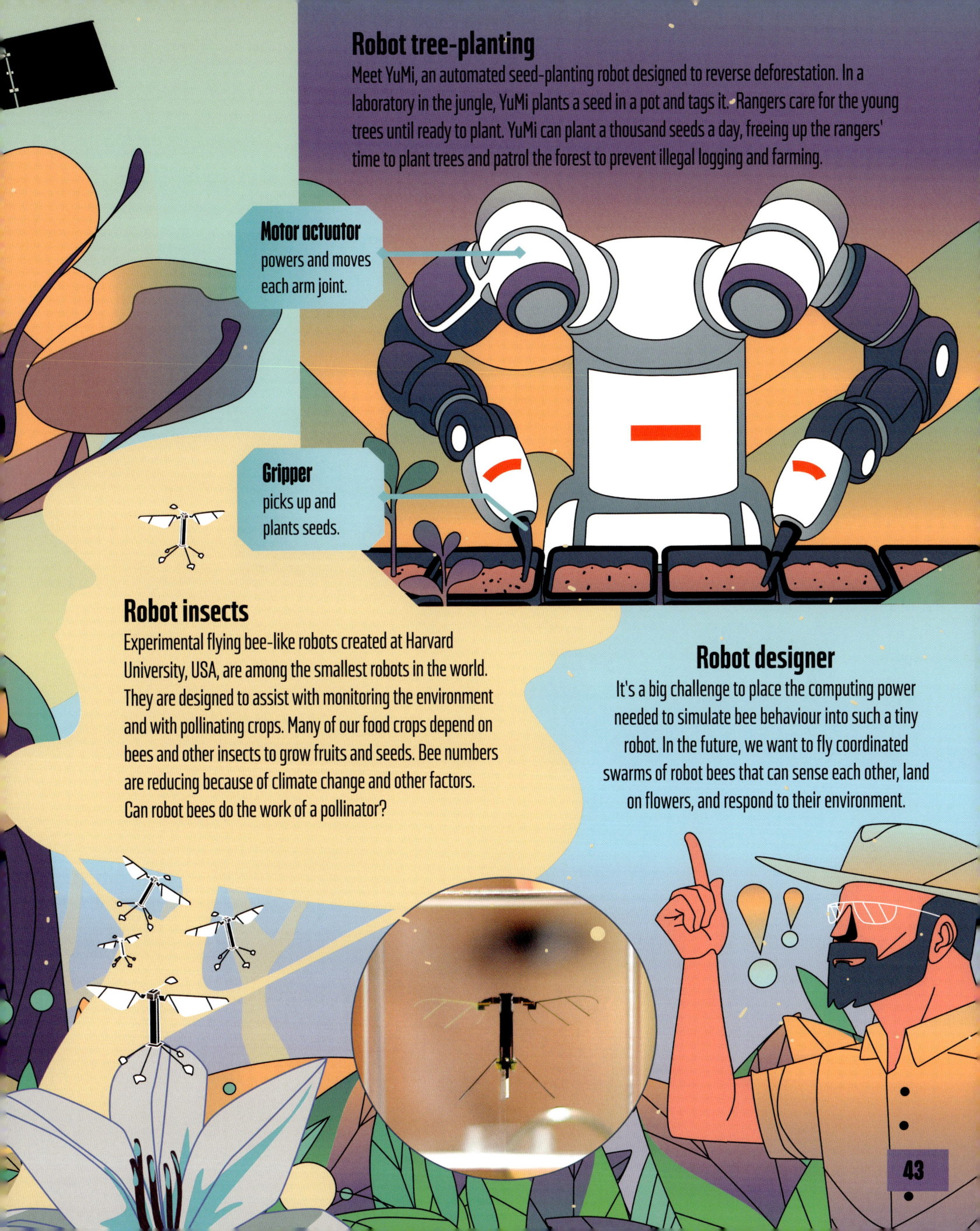

Robot tree-planting

Meet YuMi, an automated seed-planting robot designed to reverse deforestation. In a laboratory in the jungle, YuMi plants a seed in a pot and tags it. Rangers care for the young trees until ready to plant. YuMi can plant a thousand seeds a day, freeing up the rangers' time to plant trees and patrol the forest to prevent illegal logging and farming.

Motor actuator powers and moves each arm joint.

Gripper picks up and plants seeds.

Robot insects

Experimental flying bee-like robots created at Harvard University, USA, are among the smallest robots in the world. They are designed to assist with monitoring the environment and with pollinating crops. Many of our food crops depend on bees and other insects to grow fruits and seeds. Bee numbers are reducing because of climate change and other factors. Can robot bees do the work of a pollinator?

Robot designer

It's a big challenge to place the computing power needed to simulate bee behaviour into such a tiny robot. In the future, we want to fly coordinated swarms of robot bees that can sense each other, land on flowers, and respond to their environment.

Robotic animals

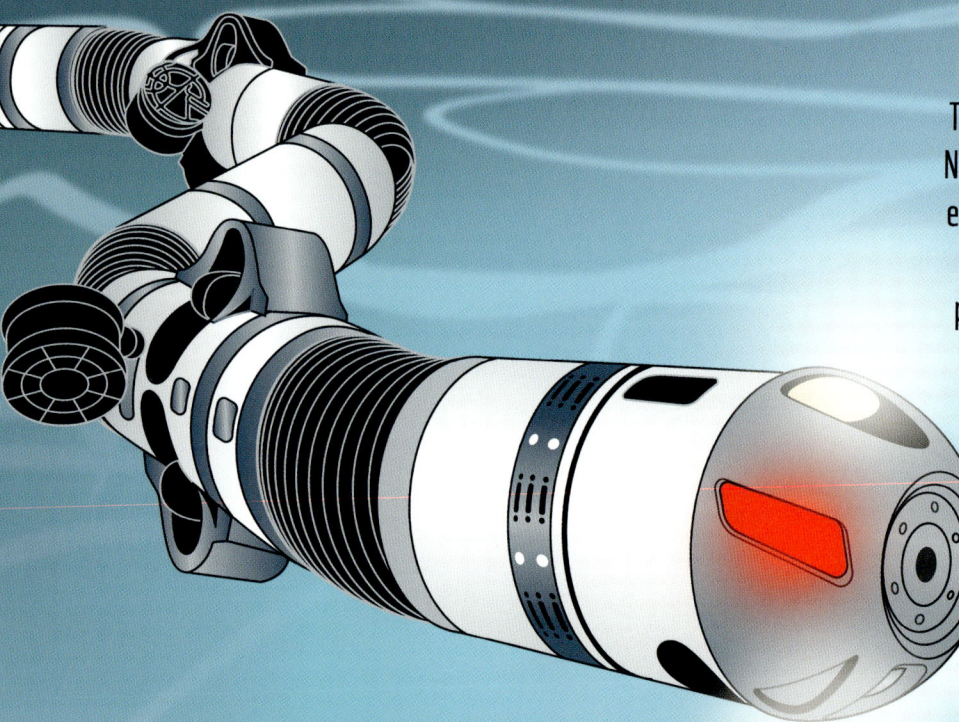

Spot
Created by Boston Dynamics, USA, Spot is a four-legged helper robot that moves like a dog and can sit, walk, crouch, go upstairs, and get up if it falls. An added arm opens doors and moves furniture. Its vision sensors record its exact position. Spot works in factories and warehouses and could one day become a home-help robot.

Eelume
This eel-like robotic arm made by Kongsberg, Norway, swims underwater and is powered by electric propellers. It's designed to travel long distances to inspect and repair underwater pipelines. When Eelume needs to send data, recharge, or change tools, it returns to its underwater docking platform.

Robotic animals

Animal bionics applies the way animals move and behave to the design of robots. The natural world inspires roboticists to create technology that enables robots to swim, fly, and to move on land in innovative ways that will assist us.

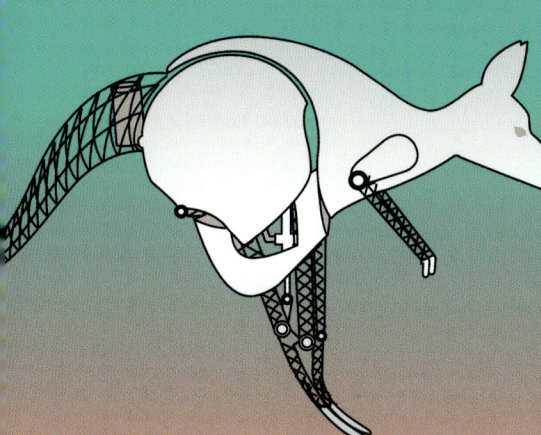

The Festo BionicKangaroo

This robot from Germany mimics the jumps of a real kangaroo! When the bionic kangaroo prepares to jump, it compresses its legs like a spring, storing energy. To jump, it rapidly releases this energy. This propels the robot into the air, mimicking the powerful leap of a kangaroo. The robot's control systems calculate the exact timing and force needed to jump and land.

The Festo BionicAnt

This robotic ant made by Festo in Germany has multiple articulated legs to crawl over different terrain, just like a real ant! The robot has cameras and tactile sensors for navigation – providing information about obstacles and surfaces to allow the bionic ant to adjust its route. A swarm of bionic ants can communicate with each other using wireless technology. This allows the group to work collaboratively, much like how ants communicate and work together in nature.

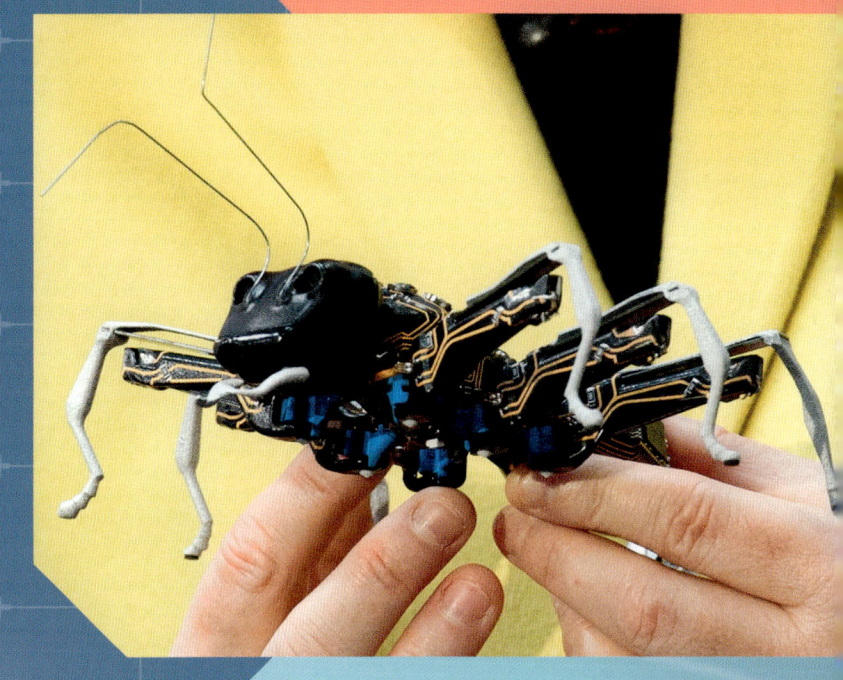

Octobot

Meet the experimental Octobot created at Harvard University, USA. Its body is made of a 3D-printed squishy silicon material. The circuits are made from liquid, rather than electric, wires. When the liquid touches the metal actuators, it turns into gas. The gas inflates the arms and makes the Octobot's tentacles move.

Spider robot

Spider robot
This robot can run and roll, just like a real-life spider called the Moroccan flic-flac. A German scientist came across this amazing animal out in the deserts of North Africa and was inspired by its movement to develop the spider robot! In the future, it may be used in farming, on the ocean floor, or on Mars.

How do robots move?

Robots have devices inside them called actuators. Just like our muscles and joints help us move parts of our body, actuators enable the robot to move and do tasks by converting energy from the robot's power source into movement. Actuators can achieve a simple movement, such as an arm moving up and down, or a more complex movement like walking.

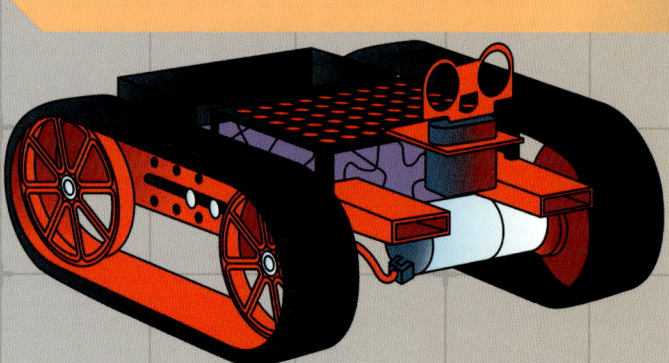

Crawling
These robots move on tracks, like tanks do. The tracks rotate in a loop powered by motors and wheels. They can grip rough, sandy, or muddy ground without getting stuck.

Wheeled
Motors power the robot's wheels. The speed of the robot depends on how fast or slow the wheels spin. A wheeled robot could travel on rails like a train or freewheel like a car.

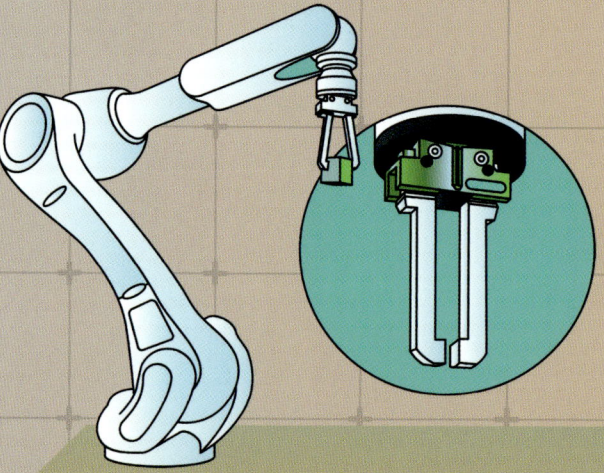

Legged movement
These robots have motors or pneumatic actuators in each leg. The robot bends and straightens its legs in a set pattern, mimicking walking or running.

Arm and gripper robots
Simple industrial robot arms do repetitive tasks, such as picking and packing, in factories and warehouses. Motors power the joints in the arm, such as an elbow or wrist. Additional motors power the gripper to pick things up. The gripper might be a simple open-and-close claw, a suction cup, or a human-like hand with multiple motors and joints in the fingers.

Flying
Hovering or flying robots include drones, aerial robots, and uncrewed aerial vehicles (UAVs). A human controls the robot from the ground with a remote-control handset. If the user wants to move the drone forwards, programing on the robot adjusts the propellers. More advanced aerial robots have AI programming to avoid collisions, control flight, and for navigation, mapping, and formation flying.

Underwater
Uncrewed underwater vehicles (UUVs) explore and map the ocean floor and underwater caves, search for sunken ships, repair power and pipelines, and monitor natural habitats. Motorized propellers move the robot in different directions, and can rotate it, too. Some robots have motorized arms and tools fitted to carry out tasks such as retrieve objects, collect samples, and perform repairs – all underwater.

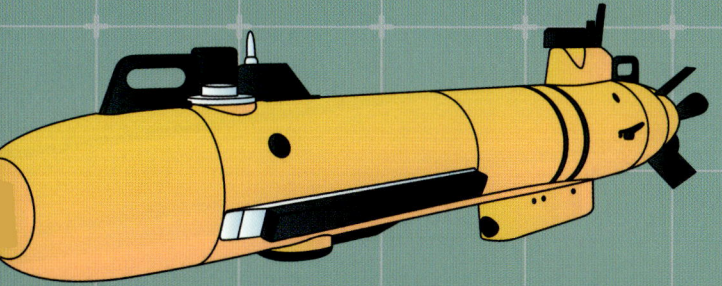

How do actuators work?

Electric actuators
Motors are common actuators in robots. They use electricity to make something spin, like a wheel, or move up and down, like an arm.

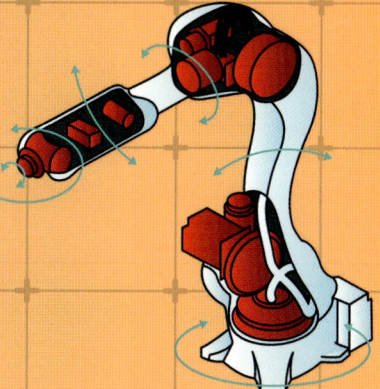

Pneumatic actuators
Compressed air (like air inside a spray can) is used to push or pull parts of the robot. When air is pumped into a cylinder, it pushes a rod out, causing movement. Pneumatic actuators can open and close a claw-like gripper to pick things up.

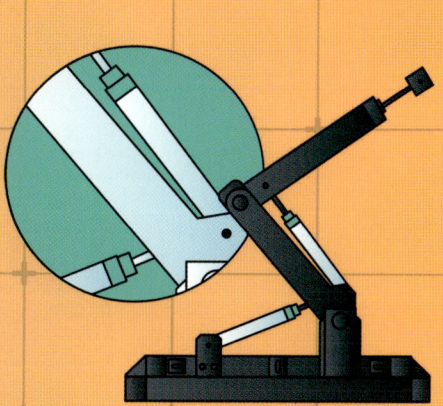

Hydraulic actuators
Pressurized liquids (like water shot from a water pistol) are used to push a piston inside a cylinder, which moves the joint. Large robot arms in factories and on construction sites use hydraulic actuators to lift heavy objects.

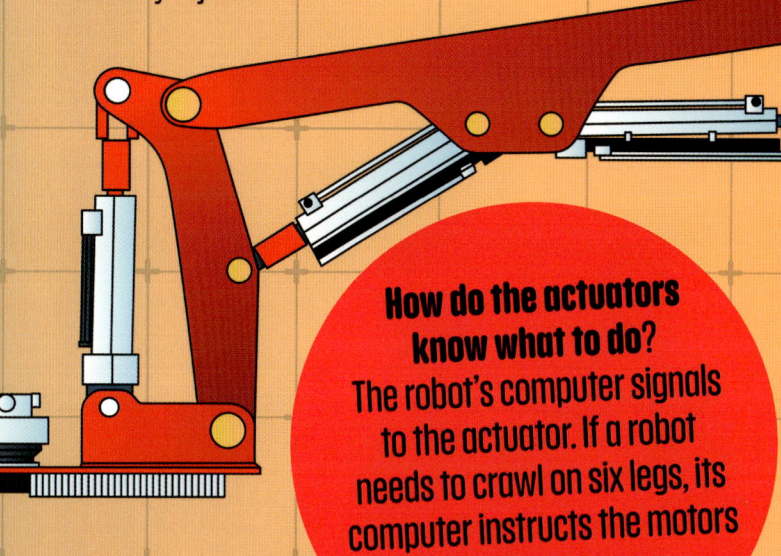

How do the actuators know what to do?
The robot's computer signals to the actuator. If a robot needs to crawl on six legs, its computer instructs the motors in the legs to move.

Military robots

Today, drones are an important part of military defence. UAVs (uncrewed aerial vehicles) are used for mapping, tracking, spying, and bombing missions. In the ocean, UUVs (uncrewed underwater vehicles) detect submarines and mines. On land, UGVs (uncrewed ground vehicles) locate bombs, and are being trialled to support soldiers by carrying heavy equipment and weapons.

I-spy drone

The MQ-9 Reaper can fly for 27 hours continuously at heights of up to 15,240 m (50,000 ft). It surveys the landscape, relaying live images of enemy activity, and carries missiles and bombs. Aircrews in ground stations pilot the drone remotely, or it can fly autonomously.

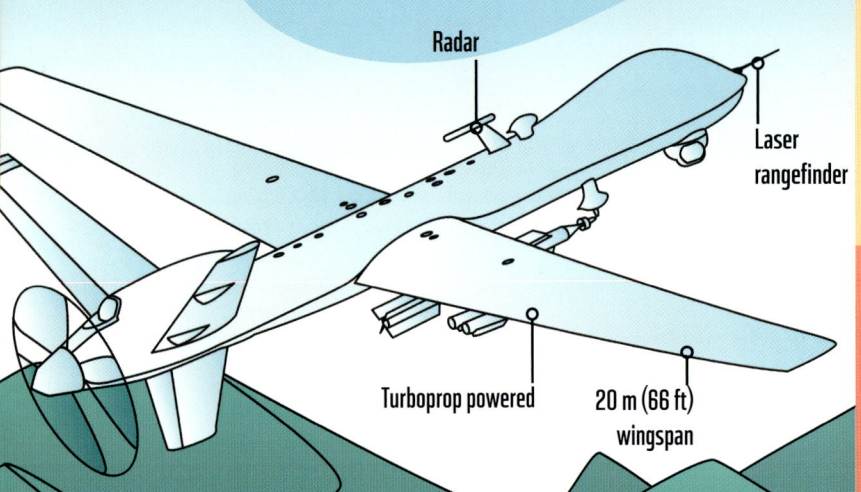

Radar
Laser rangefinder
Turboprop powered
20 m (66 ft) wingspan

Robo-tank

The Uran-9 is an unmanned ground combat vehicle with guns, a cannon, and missiles. Its operator controls the robot from a computer at a command post. The tank is used for observation and to fire on enemy positions.

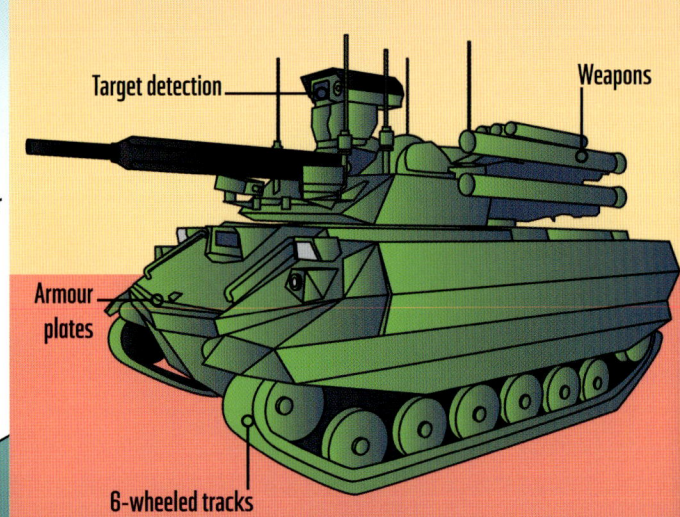

Target detection
Weapons
Armour plates
6-wheeled tracks

Minesweeper ship

A surface ship detects a mine using sonar. The ship's computer then sends commands to the mine disposal vehicle, SeaFox. Diving to depths of up to 300 m (984 ft), SeaFox uses sonar to locate the mine in the dark. It confirms the type of mine and fires a warhead to blow the mine up.

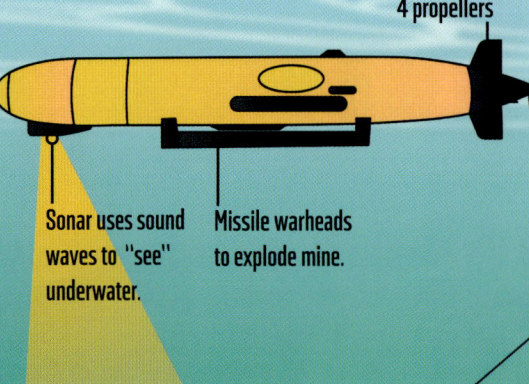

4 propellers
Sonar uses sound waves to "see" underwater.
Missile warheads to explode mine.

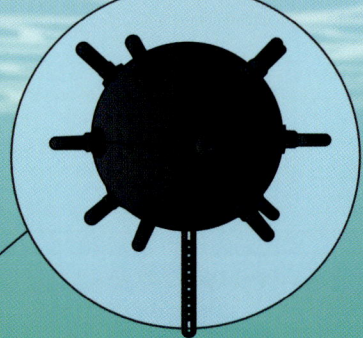

Underwater mine detection

Mines are explosive devices placed in the sea to damage and destroy ships and submarines. Some mines float on the surface, while others float midway in the water or sink to the seabed.

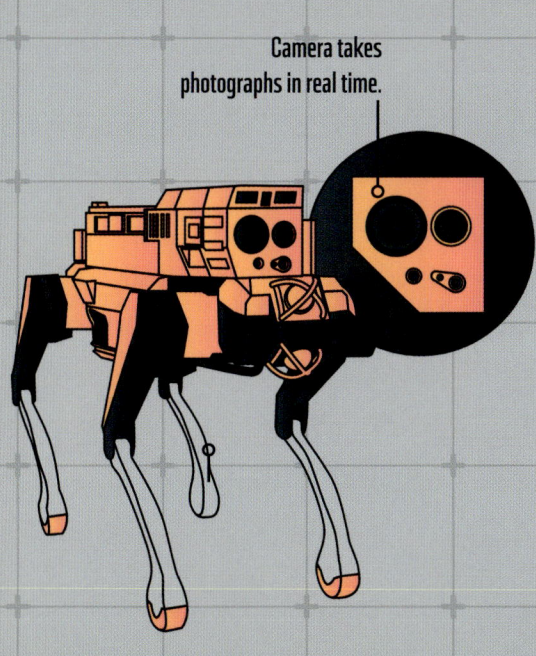
Camera takes photographs in real time.

Robo-wolf
Q-UGV Wolf is a four-legged robot designed to patrol with soldiers and carry heavy equipment and supplies on its back. It can easily move through forest and rocky terrain and responds to voice commands. It navigates autonomously or by remote control and can work in a coordinated team of robots.

Military commander
We want to remove soldiers as much as possible from dangerous missions. Our UAV and UGV robots perform risky jobs such as bomb disposal, scouting an enemy position, and even combat. Robots have advantages over humans – they don't get tired, stressed, or fearful when in danger. Robotic technology is costly, and this limits their use, but we are testing various robots to determine how they can assist. For now, an army of humanoid robot soldiers isn't part of the plan. That's still science fiction!

Border guard robots
SGR-A1 patrols the demilitarized zone along the border of North and South Korea. The robot silently guards the zone and can detect movement up to 3 km (1.9 miles) away. No one may enter or cross the zone. The robot works autonomously except for the use of weapons, which must be authorized by a human controller. If the robot detects someone, it will give verbal warnings and recognize if they are surrendering.

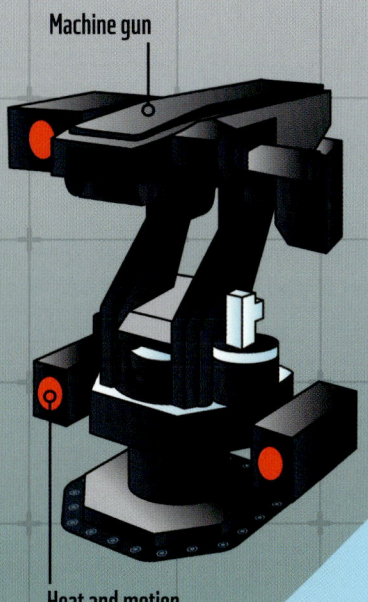
Machine gun

Heat and motion detectors

Bomb disposal
L3Harris T4 carefully approaches suspect explosive devices and views them with live cameras. Its gripper can open a suspicious bag or car boot, and a disrupter can blast open locked containers. The tracks on the robot adjust to climb stairs, navigate rocky ground, and navigate through tunnels.

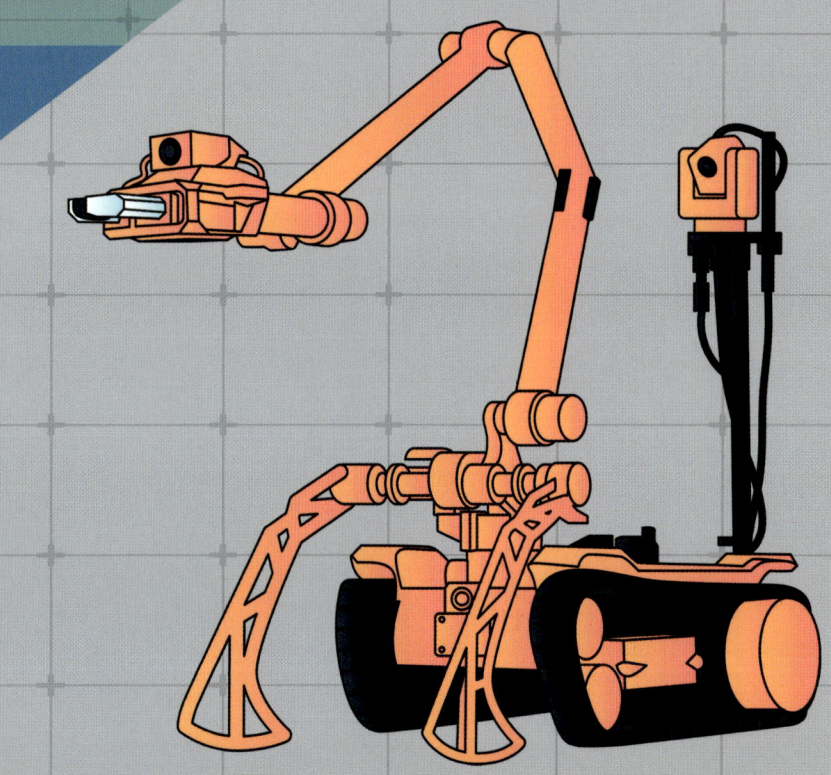

51

Search and rescue

Some robots work in places that are too risky even for emergency service people to go to, such as a collapsed building, flooded areas, and fire zones. A robot quickly monitors an area using its sensors and can deliver help and supplies to trapped or injured people.

Computer is used for AI and to avoid collisions.

8 multidirectional thrusters to help manoeuvre.

Cameras show a diver's view of the ocean.

2 arms to move, grab, and collect objects.

Force sensors relay a sense of touch to the pilot.

OceanOneK
This humanoid robot was designed by Stanford Robotics, USA, for underwater search and exploration. It can dive to 1,000 m (3,280 ft) to locate shipwrecks. Its AI works autonomously to avoid collisions, carefully handle lost treasure, and move amongst delicate reefs.

Robot engineer
From a ship on the surface, I control the robot with handheld controls and a screen. The robot's hands have a haptic feedback system, which means that I can feel shapes, textures, and objects remotely through the controls. At the same time, 3D cameras create a vision-like colour image of the underwater world.

In robotics, **an avatar is a robot version of ourselves** manipulated by programming or controls to act on our behalf.

Colossus, the firefighting robot
This robot from Shark Robotics, France, came to the rescue in April 2019, when Notre-Dame Cathedral in Paris caught fire. Colossus rolled close to the fire with a high-powered hose attached and for over 10 hours cooled the blazing inferno, saving many ancient treasures. The robot has 10 mission modules with different tools.

Firefighter
Firefighting robots can operate for hours in extreme heat, in unsafe buildings, and places with dangerous smoke, gasses, and materials. This means we can put out fires quickly without endangering firefighter safety. A trained operator remotely pilots the robot.

EMILY robot, USA
This is a remote-controlled, robotic floatation buoy that zips across the water to help struggling swimmers. EMILY has easy-to-grip handholds, and the robotic buoy tows swimmers to safety.

Robotic mining

Satellites have mapped the surface of the Earth, but what about beneath the surface? There are miles of unexplored cave systems and lava tubes. We are also searching for rare, precious elements needed to make modern-day technology. Robots are helping us to explore these hidden places and mine Earth's riches.

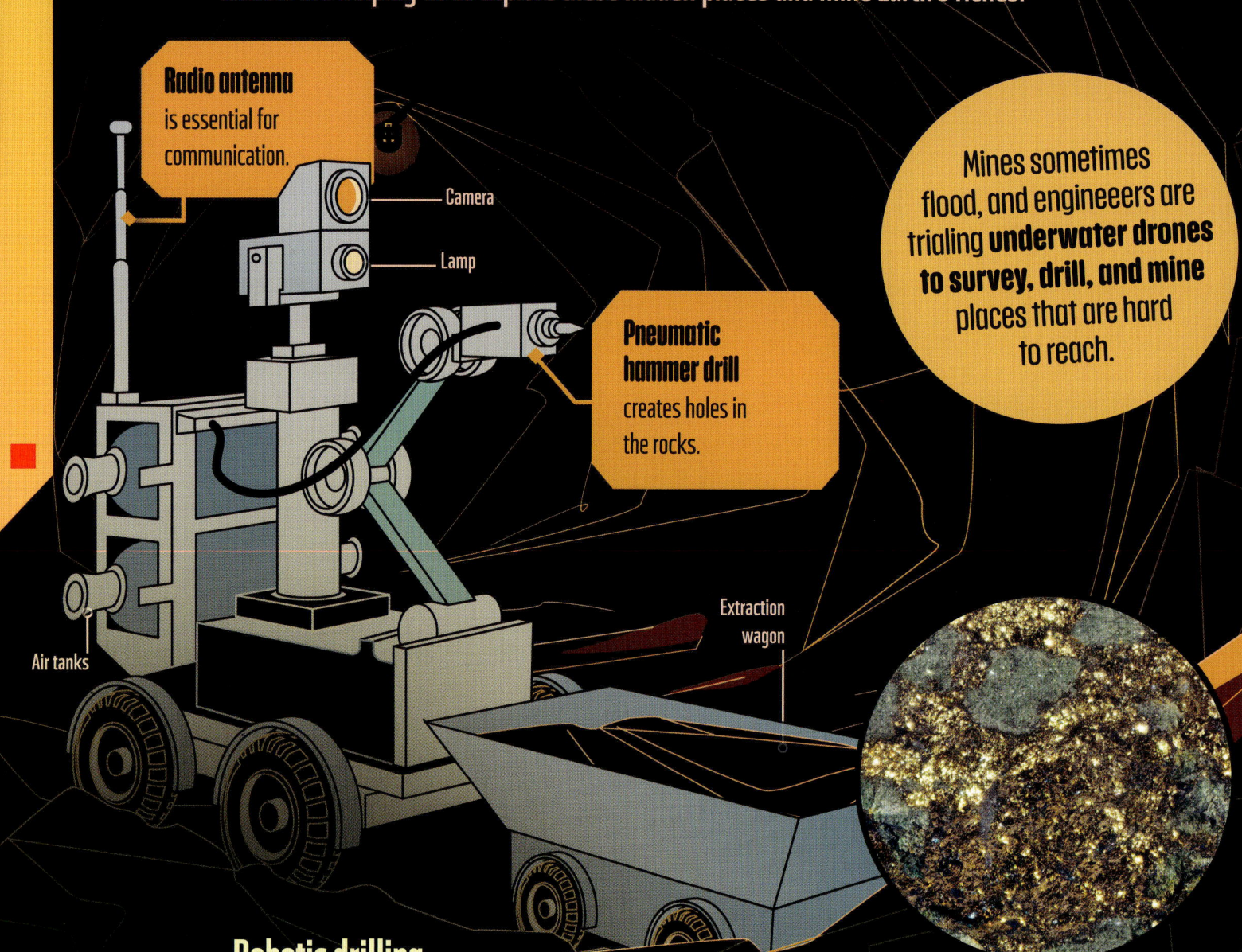

Radio antenna is essential for communication.

Camera

Lamp

Pneumatic hammer drill creates holes in the rocks.

Air tanks

Extraction wagon

Mines sometimes flood, and engineeers are trialing **underwater drones to survey, drill, and mine** places that are hard to reach.

Robotic drilling

The Rio Tinto Gudai-Darri mine in Australia operates autonomous drills to extract iron ore from the rock face. The drill's sensors detect the ore and determine where the drill hammer should strike the rock face. Autonomous trucks then load and deliver the iron ore to driverless trains that transport the ore to coastal ports for shipping.

Mining precious metals

Precious metals such as platinum, palladium, gold, and silver are used to make modern technology including computers and wind turbines. The increasing demand requires new, efficient mining methods. Surveying drones enter exploration shafts with sensors to identify minerals.

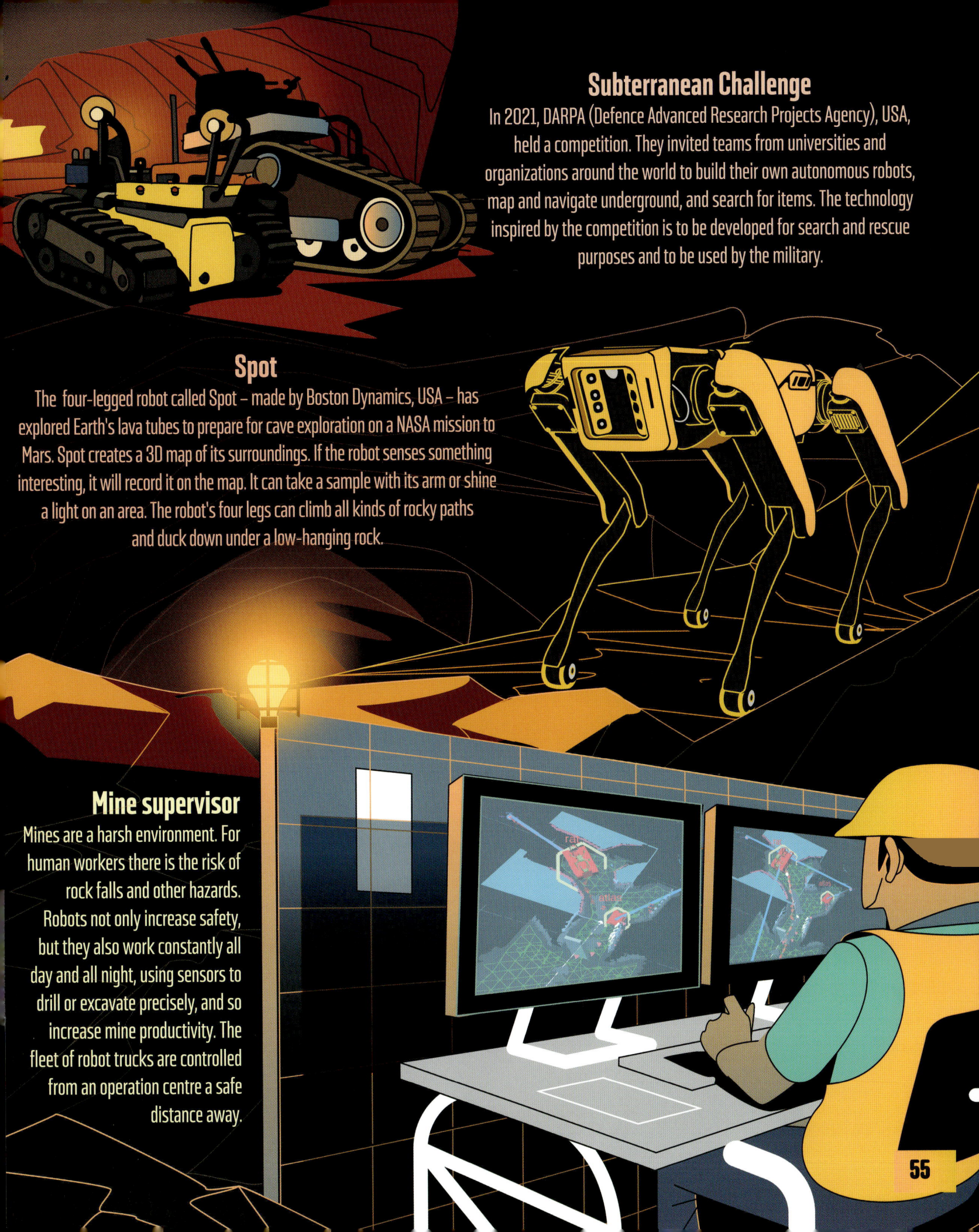

Subterranean Challenge

In 2021, DARPA (Defence Advanced Research Projects Agency), USA, held a competition. They invited teams from universities and organizations around the world to build their own autonomous robots, map and navigate underground, and search for items. The technology inspired by the competition is to be developed for search and rescue purposes and to be used by the military.

Spot

The four-legged robot called Spot – made by Boston Dynamics, USA – has explored Earth's lava tubes to prepare for cave exploration on a NASA mission to Mars. Spot creates a 3D map of its surroundings. If the robot senses something interesting, it will record it on the map. It can take a sample with its arm or shine a light on an area. The robot's four legs can climb all kinds of rocky paths and duck down under a low-hanging rock.

Mine supervisor

Mines are a harsh environment. For human workers there is the risk of rock falls and other hazards. Robots not only increase safety, but they also work constantly all day and all night, using sensors to drill or excavate precisely, and so increase mine productivity. The fleet of robot trucks are controlled from an operation centre a safe distance away.

Ocean explorers

Epipelagic zone: 0–200 m (0–650 ft)
The sunlight zone is home to much of ocean life.

Mesopelagic zone: 200–1,000 m (650–3,280 ft) This is the twilight or mid-water zone.

Ocean pressure is the amount of force from the weight of water on a given area, and it increases the deeper an object goes.

Bathypelagic zone: 1,000–4,000 m (3,280–13,120 ft)
This zone is lightless, with bioluminescent organisms.

2 multi-joint manipulator arms with adaptable force grippers to collect samples.

Abyssopelagic zone: 4,000–6,000 m (13,120–19,680 ft)
Most of the ocean floor is in this zone. Here, there are near-freezing temperatures.

Hadalpelagic zone: 6,000–10,994 m (19,680–36,000 ft)
Here, underwater canyons, called trenches, extend even deeper.

Ocean explorers

Earth's oceans are vast, and scientists estimate we haven't discovered half of Earth's marine creatures yet. The seafloor also has a varied terrain of mountains, volcanoes, valleys, and deep trenches to explore. The ocean can be divided into zones, and the pressure deep down is too great for humans to withstand without some smart submarine technology to protect us. Even then, it is not somewhere we can stay for long. It makes sense to send robots to do the exploring for us.

Mesobot
(Woods Hole Oceanographic Institute, USA)

Mission: to study water circulation and saltiness, temperature, and the creatures that swim here.

Mesobot can be remotely controlled from a surface ship via a tether, or preprogrammed to work autonomously to identify a creature and follow it. Its batteries last for 24 hours so we can see how the water and creatures change from day to night.

Slow-moving propellers help it hover and move.

Sensors study the water.

Bottles collect water.

Deep Discoverer (D2)
(NOAA Ocean Exploration, USA)

Mission: Seafloor exploration discovering new species and monitoring the ocean environment. Dives to depths of 6,000 m (19,680 ft).

Deep Discoverer (D2) has a primary camera that takes live high-definition video. It zooms in to view tiny organisms or zooms out to capture a wide view of the ocean habitat. A cable tethers the drone to the control ship. Sea creatures can be viewed through a screen in the control room.

Bottles collect water samples at different levels.

Sensors test salinity (saltiness), temperature, and oxygen levels in the water.

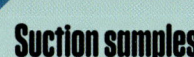

Suction samples to collect small animal and plant life.

Orpheus AUV
(Woods Hole Oceanographic Institute, USA)

Mission: Explore the terrain, and record creatures and seafloor geology.

Orpheus's streamlined shape and gentle movements allow it to glide just above the seafloor and land softly, capturing life deep down without disturbing the ecosystem.

Sensors test the water.

Glass sphere protects electronics from extreme pressure.

Underwater robots

Underwater robots

Robots can lend a hand when searching for marine animals living deep down in the water. Here employees at Yellowstone National Park, Wyoming, USA, use an underwater robot to search for invasive aquatic species.

Space robots

Rechargable batteries provide power and allow the robot to move freely in space.

32 cm (12.5 in) wide

Robotic arm grabs and holds items or grasps handrails to rest and conserve energy.

Cameras and sensors see and navigate around the station.

Air nozzles puff out pressurized air to propel the bots in any direction.

Space robots

The ISS (International Space Station) is an orbiting science laboratory the size of a six-bedroom house. Robots are helping astronauts conduct science and technology experiments in the microgravity (weightless) environment inside the space station and the vacuum of space. They are becoming valuable, time-saving assistants and can reduce astronauts' exposure to the dangers of spacewalks and exploration, and even go beyond human capabilities.

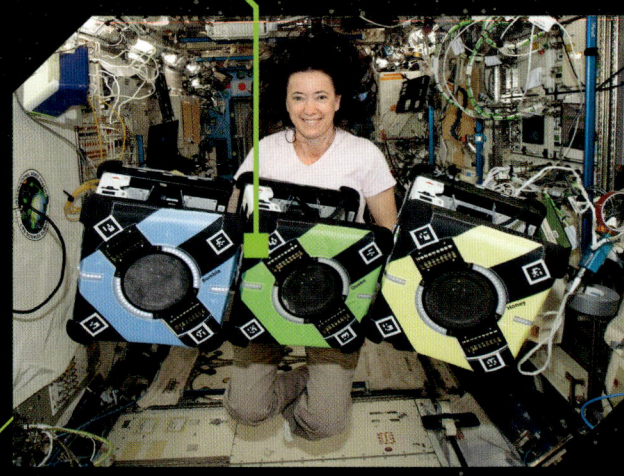

Meet the Astrobees
Free-flying cube-bots called Bumble, Harvey, and Queen arrived at the Space Station in 2019. They make 3D maps of the station's interior to navigate and do everyday tasks such as inventory checks, moving equipment, and taking live videos of science experiments to share with researchers on Earth.

What can it do?

The arm is like a giant human arm, but has rotating joints. It's mounted on a mobile base that travels along the central truss that runs the station's length. The arm can tumble end-over-end to reach many parts of the Space Station. An anchoring hand plugs into power, data, and video.

Force-movement sensors provide a sense of touch.

Three joints at the shoulder

Elbow joint

Colour cameras: two on the elbow and two on the hands.

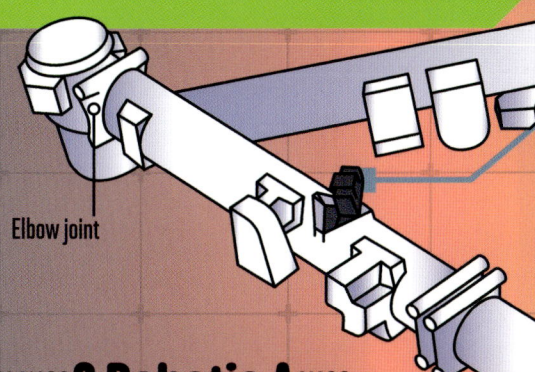

Canadarm2 Robotic Arm

This robotic arm can be controlled by mission control or astronauts inside the Space Station. **It aids astronauts on spacewalks, assists in the maintenance and repair of the station, and supports science experiments.** It is a station-builder, and can move whole modules into place. It also catches visiting spacecraft, guiding them to dock safely.

Three joints at the wrist

The arm is 17 m (56 ft) long x 35 cm (14 in) wide.

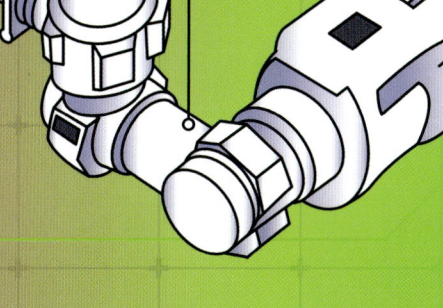

The Canadarm2 robotic arm prepares to grab the SpaceX CRS-10 Dragon cargo spacecraft, this is called a "cosmic catch".

ISS robotic operator

The controls to Canadarm2 are in the Cupola viewing window where there is a good view outside and there are also three screens that show the camera view from the arm. An operator uses hand controls to move the arm to catch a cargo spacecraft and manoeuvre it into the dock, and if there is a spacewalk outside to repair the station, the arm carries the spacewalker and tools and moves them into position.

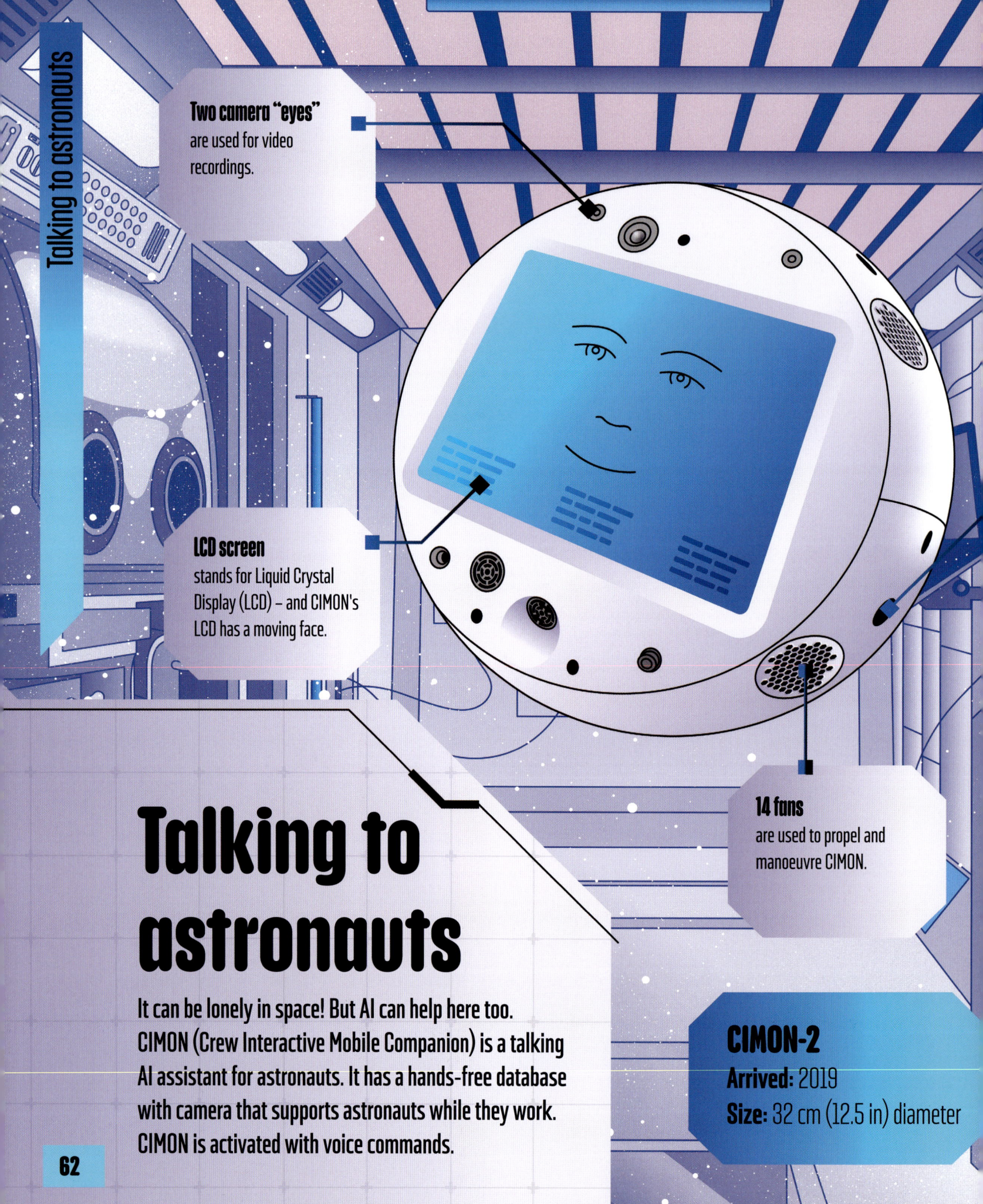

Talking to astronauts

Two camera "eyes" are used for video recordings.

LCD screen stands for Liquid Crystal Display (LCD) – and CIMON's LCD has a moving face.

14 fans are used to propel and manoeuvre CIMON.

Talking to astronauts

It can be lonely in space! But AI can help here too. CIMON (Crew Interactive Mobile Companion) is a talking AI assistant for astronauts. It has a hands-free database with camera that supports astronauts while they work. CIMON is activated with voice commands.

CIMON-2
Arrived: 2019
Size: 32 cm (12.5 in) diameter

Hello CIMON-2
CIMON talks an astronaut through how to do a task step-by-step, with visual instructions on the screen. CIMON can search and count objects, and take pictures. Robo-engineers are improving Cimon's AI to recognize facial expressions and help with more complex tasks.

Cute camera
Say hello to Int Ball! This smart little camera has joined the ISS. Developed by JAXA (Japan Aerospace Exploration Agency), it is a **camera drone that can record videos in space as it moves, governed by remote control.**

7 microphones and a direction microphone, which picks up sounds from a particular direction, are used for voice recognition.

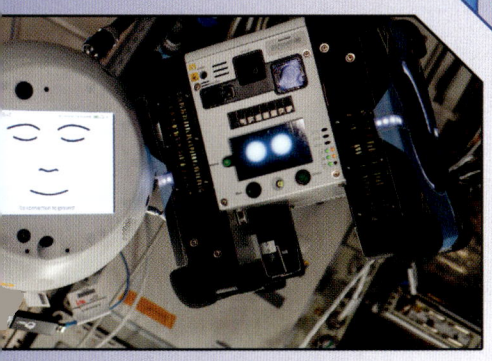

Work friends
Here, CIMON joins Bumble, one of the three Astrobees on ISS. CIMON and the Astrobees work independently on the Space Station, but both assist astronauts, support operations, and enable research that will take humans to the Moon and to Mars.

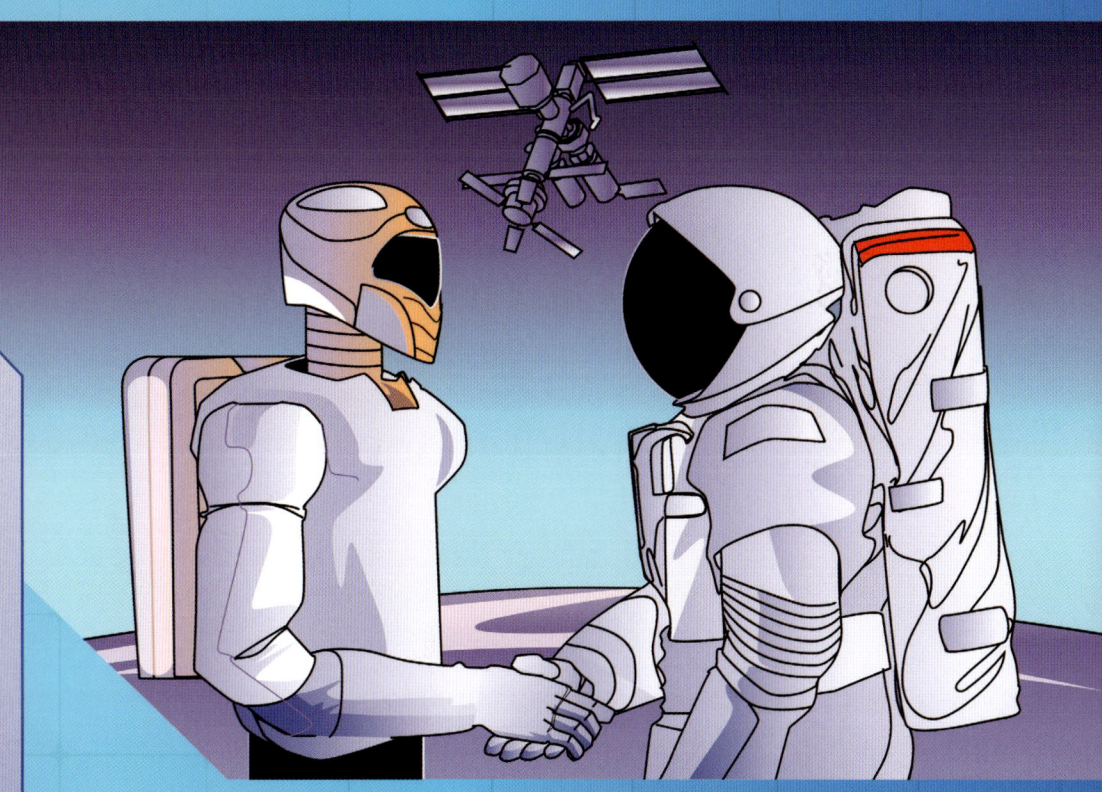

Artemis lunar mission planner
We're experimenting with advancing robots' capabilities on the ISS, ready for the launch of the Lunar Gateway, a space station that will orbit the Moon. We are investigating whether robots can become autonomous and take care of spacecraft, solve problems, and keep systems operating while the crew are away on a spacewalk or exploring a planet's surface.

Exploring Mars

Does life only exist on Earth? Or has life existed elsewhere in the Solar System? These are the BIG questions scientists are investigating with the help of robotic explorers. In February 2021, the *Perseverance* rover parachuted down to the surface of Mars and landed in the Jezero crater. Satellite images of the crater showed a dry lake and riverbed proving that water had once flowed on Mars. Scientists believe that where there was once water there could have been life.

How does it work?

The rover can either move autonomously or be operated by Mission Control. It makes decisions via an auto-navigation system. Cameras and sensors analyze the environment, identify objects and decide on a safe path across the rocky Martian terrain. Scientific instruments and AI technology identify rock and soil samples. AI sorts and selects the most relevant data to send to scientists back on Earth.

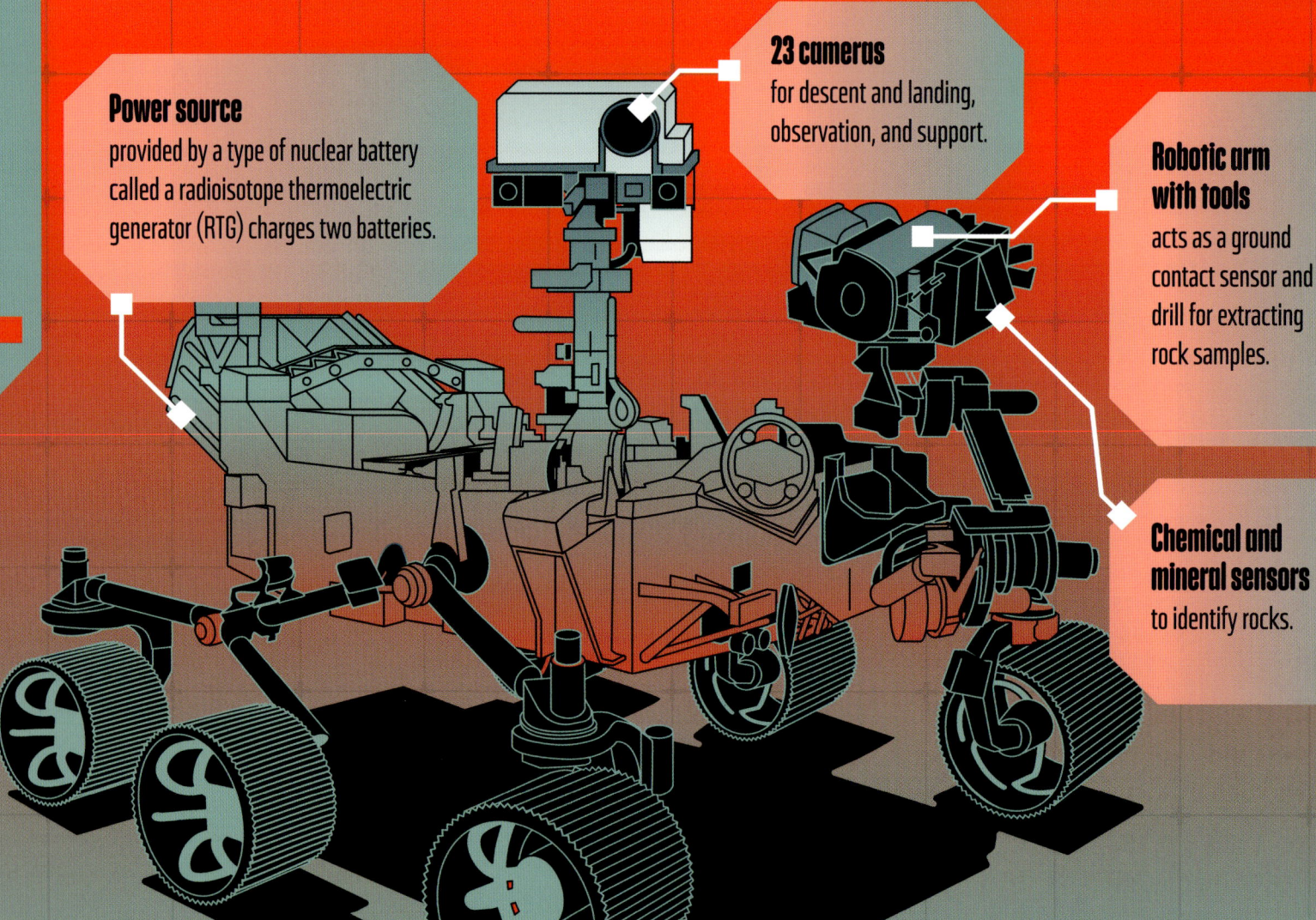

Power source provided by a type of nuclear battery called a radioisotope thermoelectric generator (RTG) charges two batteries.

23 cameras for descent and landing, observation, and support.

Robotic arm with tools acts as a ground contact sensor and drill for extracting rock samples.

Chemical and mineral sensors to identify rocks.

Computer processor monitors temperature and power, stores data, plans and makes decisions, and communicates with Earth or Mars orbiters.

Perseverance mission

The rover's mission is to search for signs of ancient life by studying and collecting rock and soil samples and to test new flight technology to assist future human exploration. Its instruments also analyze surface geology (rock structures) and Martian weather.

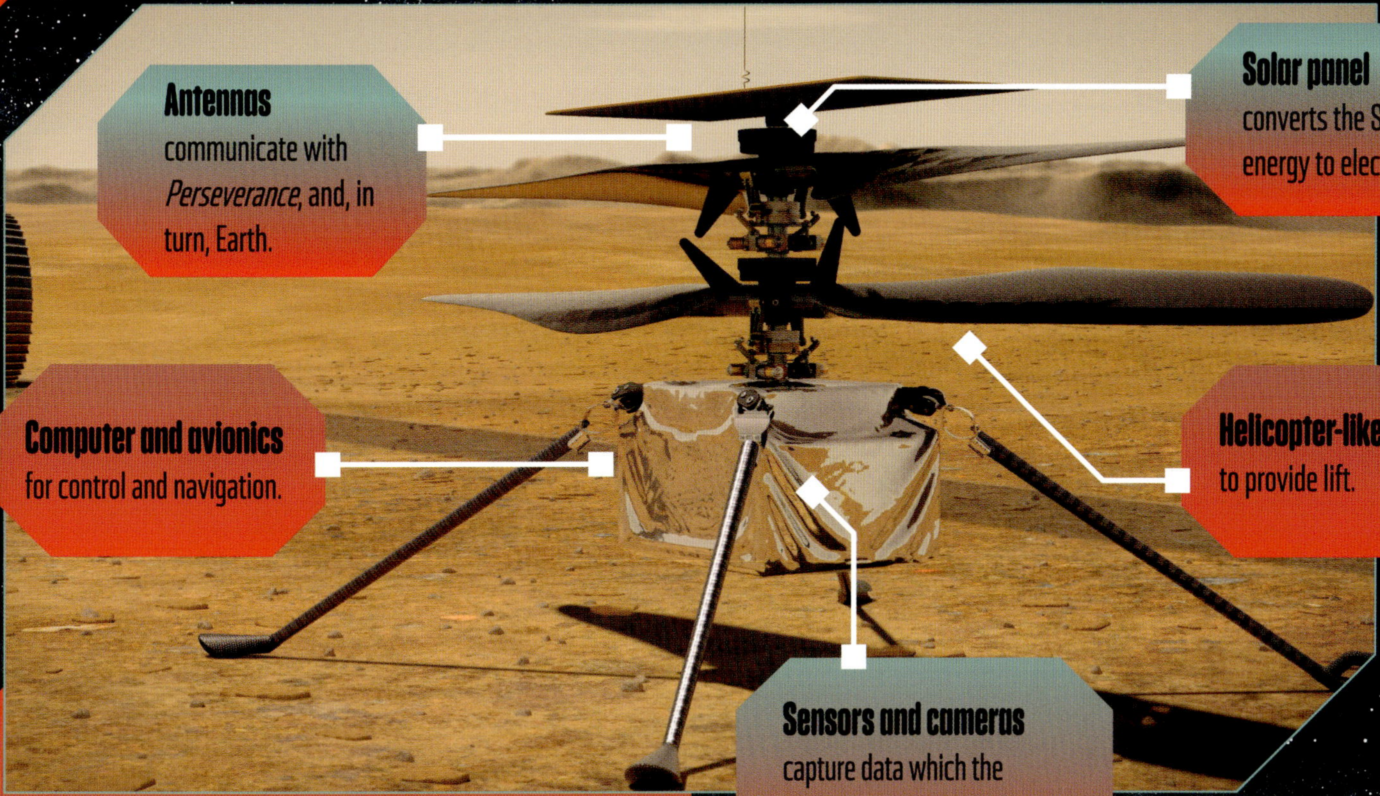

Antennas communicate with *Perseverance*, and, in turn, Earth.

Solar panel converts the Sun's energy to electricity.

Computer and avionics for control and navigation.

Helicopter-like blades to provide lift.

Sensors and cameras capture data which the computer uses to work out direction and speed.

Ingenuity misson

The *Ingenuity* helicopter arrived on Mars safely stored beneath *Perseverance*. It detached from the rover and flew 72 times over nearly three years. It is the first aircraft to achieve powered, controlled flight on another planet! *Ingenuity*'s mission was to test its flight capabilities in the very thin Martian atmosphere and to be a scout for the rover, finding areas of interest to explore.

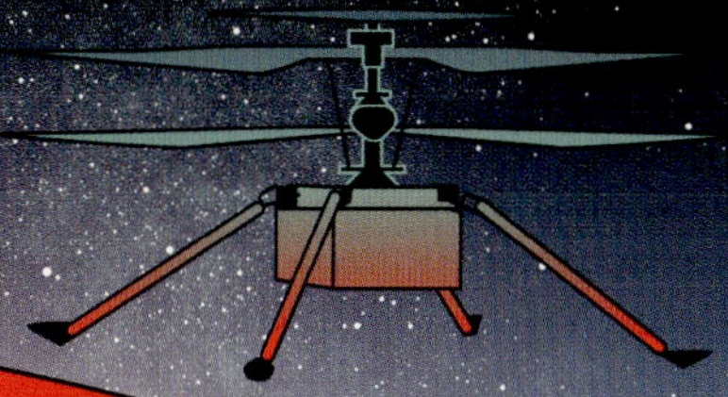

Drones

Drones will be very useful scouts during future human missions to Mars. Engineers are developing drones that could fly on other planets or moons. These drones carry cameras and science instruments, and can cover a much larger area faster than a ground rover.

Returning rocks to Earth

The rover collects rock and soil samples with its drill and stores the samples in tubes. It leaves the tubes on the Martian surface and records their location. Scientists are developing technology to enable a future robotic probe to travel to Mars, collect the samples, and return them to Earth for study.

Mission scientist

Perseverance's SHERLOC instrument analyzes rocks searching for biosignatures – signs of past plant or animal life, much like the fossils we've found on Earth. However, we need to be open-minded! Martian life forms could look very different to the life we know.

65

Space probes

Our own robotic explorers, space probes journey across the Solar System to uncover its mysteries. They study planets, moons, and asteroids collecting data that helps us understand our cosmic neighbours. With every mission, space probes bring us closer to answering questions about the Universe and our place within it.

New Horizons
NASA's New Horizons deep space probe launched in 2006. It's a robotic spacecraft that is on a mission to explore the outer reaches of the Solar System, including a mysterious **area called the Kuiper Belt, home to the dwarf planet, Pluto.**

Large antenna
used to communicate with Earth.

Power source
is provided by a type of nuclear battery called a radioisotope thermoelectric generator (RTG).

Image of Pluto taken by New Horizons.

Pluto and Charon
In 2015, New Horizons took close-up pictures of Pluto for the first time, and also passed by Charon, one of Pluto's many moons. New Horizons acts autonomously to make decisions based on preprogrammed instructions. Its distance from Earth means simple commands take about seven hours to reach the probe, plus seven hours for mission control to see if the probe has understood the instructions.

Science instruments
include cameras and spectrometers that identify the makeup of objects and observe the solar wind.

TAGSAM

NASA's OSIRIS-REx spacecraft launched in 2016 and travelled for two years to reach the asteroid Bennu. It mapped the boulder-covered surface to find a safe spot for sampling. The probe deployed a robotic arm called TAGSAM (Touch-and-Go Sample Acquisition Mechanism) to collect samples. As the spacecraft was returning to Earth, it released the sample container in orbit, which was finally parachuted to the ground for retrieval and study.

Solar panels are used to power the robotic arm.

TAGSAM robotic arm puffs air to loosen rock and dust and then sucks it into a container.

Laser altimeter for measuring the 3D shape of Bennu.

Sample return capsule is a special container used for collecting samples.

The asteroid's dust is rich in carbon and nitrogen, as well as organic compounds, including water molecules – the ingredients that formed the Solar System and are essential for life.

Kuiper Belt
The probe continues its mission in the Kuiper Belt, a region of icy, rocky objects left over from the creation of the Solar System. It identifies strange objects scientists have spotted from telescopes on Earth and measures the power of the Sun's solar rays at the edge of the Solar System.

Why study asteroids?
Asteroids are made of ancient materials that haven't changed much since the Solar System was first formed. Billions of years ago, an asteroid could have crashed on our planet's surface carrying organic molecules and water – the building blocks of life. So studying asteroids may help to answer questions about how life began on Earth.

The story of robots

These milestones highlight the amazing journey of robots – from early ideas to the first simple machines and onto the complex systems of today, which continue to shape our future.

c.1495: Design of a knight in armour, Italy
Leonardo da Vinci designed one of the first humanoid robots, a knight in armour which could sit up, wave its arms, and move its head.

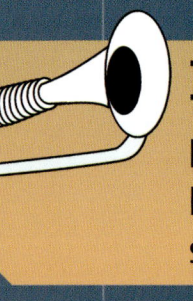

c.1739: The Digesting Duck, France
Jacques de Vaucanson built a robotic duck that could flap its wings, eat grain, and poop!

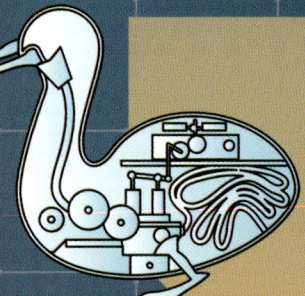

1810: First humanoid robot, Germany
Friedrich Kaufmann built a robot soldier that could blow a trumpet.

c.1820: Mechanical performance dolls, Japan
Hisashige Tanaka, founder of the technology company, Toshiba, invented mechanical puppet dolls with complex movements that inspired Japan's love of robots.

c.1920: The first use of the word "robot", Czech Republic
The word "robot" first appeared in a play called *R.U.R.: Rossum's Universal Robots*, by playwright, Karel Čapek.

1932: Lilliput, Japan
The first robot toy.

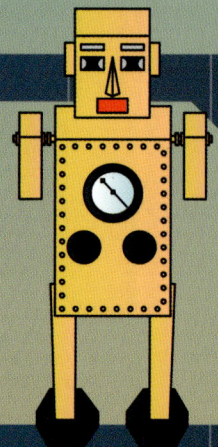

c.1949: Battery-powered tortoise, UK
W. Grey Walter built one of the first machines to navigate on its own. The robot could manoeuvre around objects and return to a charging point.

1950: The Turing Test, UK
Mathematician Alan Turing proposed a test called the Imitation Game – to see if a machine could think for itself, like a human.

1953: Unimate, USA
George Devol invented the first digitally operated and programmable industrial robot arm.

1956: First use of "Artificial Intelligence", USA
A group of "thinking machine" researchers led by mathematician Professor John McCarthy first used the term "Artificial Intelligence".

1956: The Logic Theorist – early AI program, USA
Allen Newell, J.C. Shaw, and Herbert Simon developed the program at Carnegie Institute of Technology.

1963: The Belgrade Hand, Serbia
The first robotic, prosthetic hand.

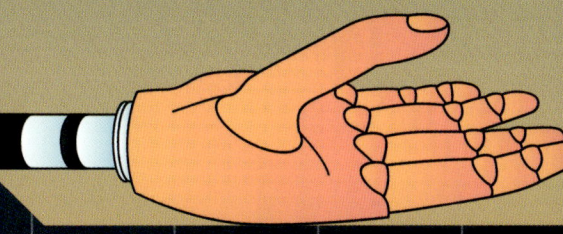

1964: IBM 360, USA
The first computer to be mass-produced.

1966: ELIZA, early chatbot, USA
Computer scientist Joseph Weizenbaum created ELIZA, one of the first chatbots.

1966–1972: Shakey, USA
Developed by the Stanford Research Institute, Shakey had multiple sensors and was the first mobile robot that could reason about its environment and make decisions based on what it "saw".

1973: Freddy, UK
The Assembly Robotics Group at Edinburgh University developed a moveable, overhead robotic arm with a gripper that could locate and assemble models.

1975: Albatross and Amber, USA
The first UAV drones.

1985: PUMA, USA
The Programmable Universal Machine for Assembly (PUMA) 200 was the first surgical robot.

1994: Dante II, USA
An eight-legged walking robot, built at Carnegie University, descended into Mount Spurr, in Alaska, to collect volcanic gas samples.

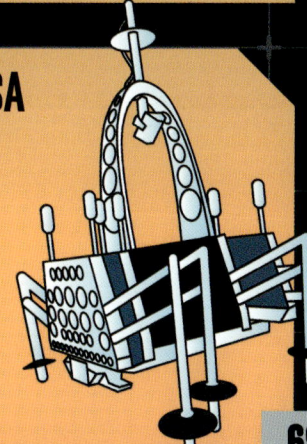

The story of robots

1996: RoboTuna, USA
David Barrett at Massachusetts Institute of Technology (MIT) developed a biometric robot resembling a fish to advance AUV propulsion.

1999: Kismet, USA
Developed by MIT, the first humanoid helper robot to recognize speech and human emotions, and engage in conversation.

1997: Deep Blue, USA
An IBM chess-playing computer program competed against the reigning world chess champion and won.

2000: ASIMO, Japan
The Advanced Step in Innovative Mobility (ASIMO) from Honda was a walking, talking humanoid designed to help people.

1997: Sojourner, NASA, USA
First autonomous rover deployed on the surface of Mars.

1990s: The first autonomous car, USA
The NavLab program at Carnegie Mellon University developed the first AV capable of driving without human intervention.

1997: First Robocup Tournament, Japan
The goal is to have a fully automated team of robots beat the world's best human soccer team by 2050.

2002: Roomba, USA
iRobot released an early robotic vacuum cleaner.

1999: Sony AIBO, Japan
A robotic dog which interprets human emotions.

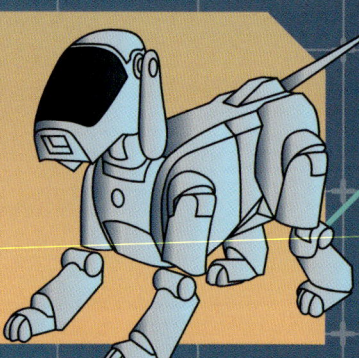

2003: Kiva the warehouse bot, USA
Kiva Systems developed the Kiva bot, and Amazon later bought the robotics company to robotize its warehouses in 2012.

2004: Micro flying robot, Japan
Epsom built a 7 cm (2.8 in) tall flying camera drone to assist with natural disasters.

2010: Big Dog, USA
An advanced mobility robot built by Boston Dynamics walks, runs, and carries heavy loads for the military over rough terrain.

2011: Siri, USA
The first commercial virtual assistant, launched on the Apple iPhone 4S.

2016: Sophia, Hong Kong
The first humanoid robot to be granted citizenship in Saudi Arabia. It was created by Hanson Robotics.

2016: Weymo, USA
The first commercial ride-share AV "robotaxis" were launched.

2020: Robots in COVID-19 response, USA
The robot, Pepper, and disinfection drones were used in hospitals and public spaces to reduce human contact and assist with social distancing measures.

2021: Ingenuity, USA
NASA launched the first robotic aircraft to conduct a controlled, extra-terrestrial flight.

2022: ChatGPT, USA
OpenAI released the prompt-based AI text generation app for public use.

2022: Optimus, USA
Tesla demonstrated this advanced humanoid robot.

2024: robotic ants, South Korea
Scientists at Hanyang University in Seoul developed swarms of tiny magnetic robots that work together like ants to lift much heavier objects and complete clever tasks.

Step into the future

Robotic technology is advancing rapidly. Advances in automation, AI, and the materials used to build robots will create increasingly capable machines that will change the way we live. Let's find out what the future holds...

Goodbye to chores
Buying a home-assistant robot is as common as buying a smart phone. AI robots can take over tidying, cleaning, cooking, organizing the home calendar, and can even help with homework too!

Your robot friend
Companion bots come in lots of shapes and sizes. Your robot pal will understand your moods and preferences and will always be there to play, chat, hug, and help solve your problems.

Smart cities
On the high street, holographic window displays and personal-shopping robots help you to choose.

High-tech vertical and rooftop farms grow food locally.

Driverless trains and buses are on time and faster.

Order a ride, and a driverless vehicle turns up! With fewer vehicles and car parks, city and town centres are greener, quieter, and safer places.

A fleet of gardening and rubbish-collection bots work day and night to keep towns and cities tidy.

Swarm robot-workers
A group of bots self-organize to do complex tasks as a team, such as construct and repair buildings, search and rescue people, care for farm crops, and remove plastic from the ocean.

Interactive home shopping
Visit a VR (virtual reality) store to choose your shopping, or see how a new outfit might suit you using AR (augmented reality). A delivery drone arrives at your door with your choices within hours.

Robots in the classroom
AI robot teaching-assistants answer students' questions, set and mark homework, and provide one-to-one tutoring. Students can practise new languages and computer coding with their classroom bot.

Nanobot healthcare
Doctors inject tiny, microscopic robots into a patient's bloodstream to deliver medicine directly to infected or damaged cells.

Supercharged human abilities
Headsets with neural interfaces connect our brain directly to AI computers and machines. This enables robotic devices to be controlled by our minds.

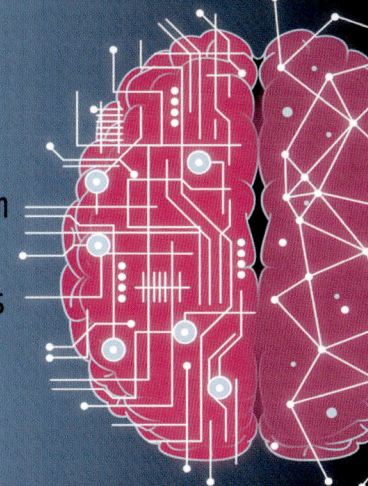

Nowhere on Earth is off-limits
Robotic explorers map cave systems, lava tubes, the ocean's seabed, and the last great wildernesses, travelling where it's too dangerous for humans to go.

The search for extraterrestrial life continues...
On Titan, Saturn's largest moon, rotor-drones survey the terrain from above while rovers and mining-bots search for life beneath the rock and surface-ice.

Live off-world!
Autonomous orbiters, rovers, drones, and assistant bots help to build and maintain a base on the Moon and Mars.

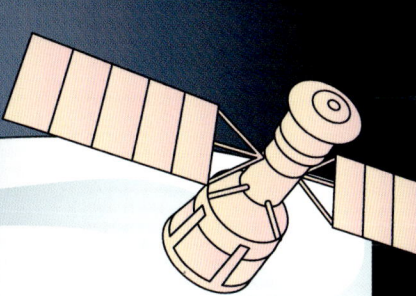

Glossary

ACCELEROMETER instrument for measuring the acceleration of a moving or vibrating body

ACTUATOR device that causes a robot or machine to move

ALGORITHM set of step-by-step instructions for performing a task, for example by a computer program

ALTIMETER instrument used to measure the height, or altitude, of an object

ARTIFICIAL INTELLIGENCE ability of computers to perform tasks that require human intelligence, such as learning and reasoning

AUTOMATED something, such as a robot, operated by a computer or machine that often does not need human control

AUTONOMOUS describes the ability to make decisions and take actions independently

BIOMETRIC describes the automated recognition of a person by their physical characteristics; it is often used in security

BIONIC having an artificial, often electromechanical, body part or parts

BOT shortened form of "robot"; also describes a software program that performs automated tasks

CHARGING STATION place where the battery of a robot or electric vehicle can be recharged

CHATBOT computer program designed to copy conversation with people, especially over the internet

COMPUTE reason or calculate

CONNECTIVITY state of being connected

DATA facts and statistics collected together for reference or analysis

DIGITAL using or relating to computer technology

DOCK piece of electrical equipment to which a portable electrical machine can be connected; also called a docking station

DRONE aircraft or flying device with no pilot

GYROSCOPE instrument that tracks orientation

HUMANOID robot that looks and moves like a human

INFRARED part of the electromagnetic spectrum with wavelengths longer than visible light, but shorter than microwaves; it is used in technology to enable devices to communicate without cables

LIDAR detection system which works on the principle of radar, but uses light from a laser

MICROGRAVITY very weak gravity

MICROWAVES form of electromagnetic radiation with wavelengths shorter than other radio waves but longer than infrared waves

NETWORK two or more linked computers that communicate electronically with each other

NEURAL relating to a nerve or the nervous system

PROGRAM set of instructions that a computer follows to complete a task

PROPRIOCEPTION awareness, or perception, of the position and movement of the body

RADAR detection system that bounces radio waves off an object; used in mapping and to locate aircraft and ships

RADIATION invisible rays of energy, such as X-rays

RECHARGEABLE describes a battery or battery-operated device that has its electrical energy restored by connection to a power supply

ROBOTICIST expert in the field of robotics

ROBOTICS design, building, operation, and use of robots

SENSOR instrument that collects data about an object

SIMULATOR device or program that imitates a real-life process or system

SMART TECHNOLOGY describes electronic devices that use systems, such as AI, to complete tasks efficiently

SOFTWARE programs on a computer that tell it how to work

SPECTROMETER instrument that separates emitted or reflected light (spectra) into a rainbow of colours that show what an object is made of

TACTILE relating to touch

TRUSS framework, typically consisting of rafters, posts, and struts, supporting a roof, bridge, or other structure

ULTRASONIC sound with vibrations greater than the upper limit of the hearing range for humans

ABBREVIATIONS:

AI Artificial Intelligence
AR Augmented Reality
AUV Autonomous Underwater Vehicle
AV Autonomous Vehicle
CIMON Crew Interactive Mobile Companion
GPT Generative Pre-training Transformer
GPU Graphical Processing Unit
IoT Internet of Things
ISS International Space Station
JAXA Japan Aerospace Exploration Agency
LCD Liquid Crystal Display
LED Light Emitting Diode
LIDAR Light Detection and Ranging
NASA National Aeronautics and Space Administration
NOAA National Oceanic and Atmospheric Administration
RADAR Radio Detection and Ranging
RTG Radioisotope Thermoelectric Generator
SCARA Selective Compliance Articulated Robot Arm
SONAR Sound Navigation and Ranging
TAGSAM Touch-and-Go Sample Acquisition Mechanism
UAV Uncrewed Aerial Vehicle
UGV Uncrewed Ground Vehicle
UUV Uncrewed Underwater Vehicle
UV Ultra Violet
VR Virtual Reality

INDEX

A
actuators 7, 48, 49
Aibo 38
Amazon 12
animals
  marine 56–57, 58
  robotic 44–47
  tracking endangered 42
antennas 65, 66
ants, robotic 45, 71
Artemis program 63
artificial intelligence (AI) 5, 8, 11, 16–17, 35, 36, 37, 69
assembly lines 24–25
asteroids 66, 67
Astrobees 60, 63
astronauts 60–63
augmented reality (AR) 39
automated robots 7
autonomous robots 7
autonomous underwater vehicles (AUVs) 56–59
autonomous vehicles (AVs) 8–11, 21, 23, 70

B
batteries, rechargeable 7, 60, 66
bees, robotic 43
Big Data 17
bionic technology 32–33, 69
bomb disposal 51
border guard robots 51
buoys, robotic 53

C
cameras 9, 12, 29, 60, 61, 62, 63, 64, 65
Canadarm2 61
cancer treatment 30, 31
Čapek, Karel 5, 68
Captcha 37
cars, autonomous 8–9
cattle farming 21
Charon 66
ChatGPT/chatbots 37, 69, 71
CIMON-2 62–63
cities, smart 72
Clearbot 41
Click-bot 39
climate change 40, 43
cobots (collaborative robots) 26–27
Colossus 53
companion bots 38, 62, 72
computer vision 17
computers 6, 9, 12, 16, 32, 69
conservation 40–43
control centres 10, 11
coral reefs 40, 41
couriers, robot 15

crawling 48
crops 18–23, 43, 73
customization 26
Cyberknife 31

D
Da Vinci robot 30–31
Deep Discovery (D2) 57
deep learning 16
disabled people 30, 32
drilling 54
driverless vehicles 8–11, 72
drones 42, 49, 65, 69
    camera 63
    delivery 15
    military 50
    surveying 20, 54

E
Eelume 44
EksoNR 32
electric actuators 49
EMILY robot 53
energy sources 7, 65, 66
engineers, robotic 52
exoskeletons 32, 33
explorers, robotic 64–65

F
facial expressions, recognition of 63
farming 18–23, 43, 73
firefighting 53
flight 49
food 18–21, 43

G
gaming chairs 39
Graphical Processing Unit (GPU) 17
gripper robots 48

H
hand-eye coordination 27
hearing 28
Hercules 13
home robots 34–35, 72
hospitals 30–31, 71
humanoid robots 6–7, 14, 27, 36–37, 68, 70, 71
hydraulic actuators 24, 40, 49

I
industrial robots 24–27
Ingenuity helicopter 65, 71
insects, robotic 43
Int Ball 63

International Space Station (ISS) 60, 61, 63
internet 35, 37

J
jellyfish robot 40

K
kangaroo, bionic 45
Kuiper Belt 66, 67

L
labour shortages 27
land conservation 42–43
Lavalboat 41
lawn mowers, robot 34
legs 48
Leonardo da Vinci 68
Lidar (Light Detection and Ranging) 8, 12, 20
life, extraterrestrial 64, 65, 73
limbs, bionic 32–33
livestock management 21
Lunar Gateway 63

M

machine learning 16
Mars 63, 64–65, 70, 73
medical robots 30–31, 71, 73
Mesobot 57
metro systems 10–11
military robots 50–51, 55
mind-controlled robotic
    devices 73
mine detection 50
mining, robotic 54–55
Moon 63, 73
movement 48–49

N

nanobots 73
Nao 37
Natural Language Processing
    (NLP) 17
navigation 12, 29, 45, 49, 51,
    55, 60, 64, 65, 68
neural interfaces 33
New Horizons space probe 66

O

OceanOneK 52
oceans
    conservation 40–41
    exploring 56–59
Octobot 45
Optimus-Gen2 36
Orpheus AUV 57
OSIRIS-REx spacecraft 67

P

Paro 38
Peppa 14
Perseverance rover 64, 65
plastic pollution 40, 73
Pleo 38
Pluto 66
pneumatic actuators 48, 49
pollination 43
pollution 40, 41
pressure sensors 28
proprioception 28
Proteus 12

R

radar 9
radiation 31
radioisotope thermoelectric
    generator (RTG) 66
remote control 49, 51, 53, 63
robotic arms 24–25, 48, 60,
    61, 64, 67, 68, 69

S

safety
    military 50–51
    mining 54–55
    search and rescue
        52–53
    space 60, 64
    workplace 33
samples, collecting 49, 55,
    56–57, 64, 65, 67, 69
satellites 42, 54
search and rescue 52–53,
    55, 71
sensors 7, 8, 28–29, 32, 60,
    61, 64, 65, 69
SHERLOC instrument 65
shopping 14–15, 73
sight 29

Siri 35, 71
smart technology 6, 16, 35, 72
smell 29
solar panels 7, 65, 67
Solar System 66–67
space probes 66–67
space robots 60–67, 73
Sparrow 13
speech recognition 28, 37, 70
spider robot 46–47
Spot 44, 55
stock management 15
store managers 15
surgery 30–31
swarm robotics 73

T

tanks, robotic 50
taste 29
taxis, ride-share 8, 71
teaching robots 37, 73
technicians, robot 13
Titan 13
touch 28
toys, robotic 38–39, 68
tractors, autonomous 21
trains, autonomous 10–11, 72
tree-planting, robot 43

Tug robot 31
Turing Test 68

U

ultrasonic sensors 28
uncrewed aerial vehicles (UAVs) 50, 51, 69
uncrewed ground vehicles (UGVs) 50, 51
underwater robots 56–9
Unitree G1 36
unmanned underwater robots (UUVs) 49

V

vacuum cleaners, robot 34, 70
vehicle manufacture 24–27
vertical farming 18–19, 72
virtual AI assistants 35
virtual reality (VR) 39
voice commands 27, 28, 51, 62

W

warehouses 12–13, 44, 48, 70
wheeled robots 48
window-cleaners, robot 35

X

Xenex 31

Y

YuMi 43

ACKNOWLEDGEMENTS

About the illustrator

Denis Freitas is an illustrator and graphic designer from São Paulo, Brazil. He has always loved cartoons and comic books, and he started reproducing the characters he liked the most and acquiring knowledge of his own through books, magazines, and practicing observation drawing. In addition to his work as an illustrator, he is also part of the Street Art duo B-47sa, producing murals and canvases since 1999.

About the consultants

Our two consultants are based at the Oxford Robotics Institute: Maurice Fallon (IEEE, Senior Member) is an Associate Professor in Engineering Science, and a Royal Society University Research Fellow. Jared Bellingham is the Lead Robotics Software and Systems Engineer.

The publisher would like to thank:
Abi Maxwell for editorial support; Kit Lane for additional design; Phil Hunt for proofreading, and Helen Peters for the index.

About the author

Kate Peridot writes both fiction and non-fiction children's titles, and likes to imaginatively blend the two to create immersive books. Kate hopes to inspire children to find out more about robots, seeing them as more than just tools, but as smart helpers and collaborators too. Kate's research skills were honed by a love of books, a sense of adventure and a fearless approach to conquering the unknown. Kate has worked as a marketer for food companies, a press officer, and a freelance writer for magazines. She now focuses on her favourite job – dreaming up and creating lots of different types of children's books. She is a member of SCBWI and SOA.

Find out more at kateperidot.com

The author would like to thank:
Becky Bagnell, my agent, for her guidance and finding the right publishing home for *Robotics*. My husband, Peter, for scanning the news and sharing clips of the latest robot tech, and lending his engineer's point of view.

Picture Credits:

The publisher would like to thank the following for their kind permission to reproduce their photographs:
(Key: a-above; b-below/bottom; c-centre; f-far; l-left; r-right; t-top)

4-5 Shutterstock.com: Evgeny Haritonov. **7 Dreamstime.com:** Thomas Lukassek (cra). **Getty Images:** Bloomberg (br). **9 Adobe Stock:** Heidi (clb). **Getty Images / iStock:** Chiociolla (tl). **10 Alamy Stock Photo:** Greg Balfour Evans (bc). **11 Alamy Stock Photo:** GALA Images ARCHIVE (bl). **14 Alamy Stock Photo:** Xinhua / Aurelien Morissard (bl). **18 Alamy Stock Photo:** Jiraroj Praditcharoenkul (cra). **20 Science Photo Library:** University Of Cambridge Collection Of Aerial Photographs (c). **21 Alamy Stock Photo:** The Bold Bureau (crb). **22-23 Alamy Stock Photo:** Suwin Puengsamrong. **24 Dreamstime.com:** Roncivil (cb). **Getty Images:** Visual China Group (crb). **25 Dreamstime.com:** Prasit Rodphan (crb). **Shutterstock.com:** Aleksandra Suzi (clb). **27 Dreamstime.com:** Aleksei Gorodenkov (br). **28 Alamy Stock Photo:** Pacific Press Media Production Corp. / Laura Chiesa (bl). **31 Alamy Stock Photo:** Hugh Nutt Photography (tc). **Getty Images:** Boston Globe (c). **Getty Images / iStock:** E+ / Sean Anthony Eddy (bc). **33 Dreamstime.com:** Framestock Footages (cla). **34 Getty Images / iStock:** HenrikNorway (cra). **37 Dreamstime.com:** Tixtis (tc). **38 Shutterstock.com:** Stefan Lambauer (tr). **39 Dreamstime.com:** Wachiwit (crb). **42-43 Alamy Stock Photo:** NASA Image Collection (tc). **43 Alamy Stock Photo:** Xinhua / © Yue Yuewei (bc). **44 Alamy Stock Photo:** CTK / Vit Simanek (tl). **45 Alamy Stock Photo:** DPA Picture Alliance / Julian Stratenschulte (cr). **46-47 Alamy Stock Photo:** DPA Picture Alliance. **48 Dreamstime.com:** Kawee Wateesatogkij (clb). **49 Alamy Stock Photo:** Olga Volodina (tl). **53 Alamy Stock Photo:** Forget Patrick (ca). **54 Alamy Stock Photo:** Phil Degginger (crb). **58-59 Alamy Stock Photo:** NPS Photo / Brett Seymour. **60 Alamy Stock Photo:** DPA Picture Alliance / NASA via CNP (crb). **61 Alamy Stock Photo:** NASA Photo / Planetpix (br). **63 Alamy Stock Photo:** JAXA / NASA / UPI (tr). **NASA:** Kayla Barron (clb). **65 NASA:** JPL-Caltech (t). **66 Alamy Stock Photo:** NASA / JHUAPL / SwRI / Futuras Fotos (clb). **67 Alamy Stock Photo:** Stocktrek Images, Inc. / Adrian Mann (ca)

Cover images: Front: **Depositphotos Inc:** Macor cra, Vetkit cl; **Dreamstime.com:** Kawee Wateesatogkij bc; Back: **Alamy Stock Photo:** JAXA / NASA / UPI cla; **Shutterstock.com:** Stefan Lambauer crb